LIVING LIFE
THE STORY OF THE
EXCEPTIONAL
ENTREPRENEUR

LIVING LIFE
THE STORY OF THE
EXCEPTIONAL
ENTREPRENEUR

Written by Ed Mlodzik based on the life of Eddie Crouch

www.MlodzikandCrouch.com

Cover design and production by Donna King
www.creativecounts.com

PUBLISHING 2014

First Printing: 2014

ISBN-13: 978-0692314906
ISBN-10: 0692314903

E.E. Publishing
6308 W. 100th Terrace
Overland Park, KS 66212
www.mlodzikandcrouch.com

Ordering Information:

Special discounts are available on quantity purchases by corporations, associations, educators, and others. For details, contact the publisher at the above listed address or at www.mlodzikandcrouch.com.

U.S. trade bookstores and wholesalers: Please contact Ed Mlodzik at (913) 706-6011 or email ed@mlodzikandcrouch.com.

Dedication

To my lovely wife, Bea Mlodzik,

Thank you. Without your support and patience,
I would have never achieved my dream.

To Donna King, my program manager,
editor, designer, marketer, and friend,

Thank you for your diligence and attention to detail.

"Living Life The Story of an Exceptional Entrepreneur
is not only an accurate account of Eddie's business career but also
a valuable resource to help others who want to start and lead a
business! No one knows more about the ups and downs of
business start-ups than Eddie Crouch"
~ *Jack Wylie, Business Partner & Investor*

Contents

Acknowledgements

Many of the tools and techniques found in the Competency Development Section (Pages 65 – 127) of this book were the result of working with a highly creative team of coaches at Sprint Corporation – a team that I was honored and proud to lead. Our staff meetings focused on how to help executives become more effective and *exceptional* leaders. I'd like to give a heartfelt thanks to Deb Amandola, Susann Arseth, John Klein, Joan Lightsey, Tom Patterson, Peg Peterson, Bob Schaumburg, Johanna Rowan, Cindy Swall, Mickie Schroeder, and Rich Tufarolo - all talented, professional coaches that I highly recommend to anyone interested in developing their leadership skills and talents.

At Sprint, I also had the opportunity to see many leaders apply their skills in starting and leading initiatives. I would like to specifically thank the following leaders who consistently applied leadership values and behaviors to their work. Like Eddie Crouch, *The Exceptional Entrepreneur*, they exhibit the *Exceptional Dimensions* outlined in this book and are truly great leaders. Thank you Alana and Mike for setting a good example!

Alana Muller, Former Director at University of Excellence at Sprint, Past President of Kauffman FastTrac, Master Networker and Author of the book, *Coffee Lunch Coffee: A Practical Field Guide for Master Networking*

Mike Hennigan, Vice President of Site Development at Sprint

Foreword

The entire process of working with the author, Ed Mlodzik, has been an exciting, powerful, and spiritual experience prompting a sense of thankfulness of all the blessings I have received.

Reflecting on life and recounting past situations, both good and bad, has given me the opportunity to think about my life, my businesses, and most importantly, my relationships with family and friends.

I would like to thank my wife, Patsy, for her unyielding support, guidance, and faith, as well as my entire family for being involved in my life and my business career. I am *exceptional* because of you!

This book is a great tool for anyone who wants to develop the competencies to be successful not only as an entrepreneur, or in business, but also in life. I wish I had a helpful "guide" like this when I started in business. Being able to contribute and share my learnings and knowledge is a way for me to give back and pay forward.

Thank you, Ed, for recognizing the *Exceptional Dimensions* in me and writing this book to help others turn their dreams into reality. I am honored to be *The Exceptional Entrepreneur and I am Living Life!*

Eddie Crouch
November 2014

Preface

This book is an approach to the study of leadership in a unique way. It is NOT a book exclusively about leadership. It is NOT a book exclusively about an entrepreneur. It is both!

This is a story about the business life (still going on) of what I call an *Exceptional Entrepreneur*. This is a real story of how a man (Eddie Crouch {rhymes with Couch}) identified opportunities and turned those opportunities into businesses. Throughout his story he consistently demonstrates certain *Exceptional Dimensions* (behaviors, characteristics, and practices) that contributed to his success (or in the case of a business setback, what dimensions were missing or ignored).

Each segment in the business career of Eddie Crouch is punctuated by exhibiting these behaviors that translate into the *Exceptional Dimensions* seen on pages 16 and 17. As you read through Eddie's story, an example of an *Exceptional Dimension* will be highlighted by one of these "boxes". Please refer to the page number referenced in the Competency Development Section of this book (Pages 65-127) to find not only a definition of the dimensions, but also specific suggestions and tools for you to use to develop that competency.

The Competency Section consists of a collection of developmental tools, techniques, and suggestions created and used by my coaching team when I was an Executive Coach at Sprint Corporation. Also included are ideas from several noted authors on these topics referenced on page 132. All provide a diverse set of approaches to apply to your professional development.

Hence, the purpose of this book is to give a student of business (in school or in the business world today) a roadmap that shows how to uncover opportunities and how to capitalize on them. Perhaps this will inspire some to create businesses and be an *Exceptional Entrepreneur*. But at the very least, a reader can assess where she/he is in their career and what development areas might need attention to advance that career, no matter what industry.

It's an adventure! And as in life, there are no guarantees.

The verse that follows best summarizes a formula for success in life. Eddie has been and is living his life this way!

"The road to success is not straight.
There is a curb called failure, a loop called confusion;
speed bumps called Friends; red lights called enemies;
caution lights called family. You will have flats called jobs.
But if you have a spare called Determination;
and engine called Perseverance; insurance called Faith,
and a driver called Jesus,
you will make it to a place called success"

~ Anonymous

The Exceptional Dimensions

EXCEPTIONAL DIMENSION #1
Building Relationships

The key is to listen first and then deliver on what you heard!

See page 76 to learn more.

EXCEPTIONAL DIMENSION #2
Visionary

The key is to create a picture of what success looks like and then build a plan to achieve it!

See page 80 to learn more.

EXCEPTIONAL DIMENSION #3
Communication

The key is consistency, impact, and clarity: consider what, who, when, where, and how your communications will be delivered most effectively!

See page 85 to learn more.

EXCEPTIONAL DIMENSION #4
Decision-making

The key is to make your decision sound and do it rapidly!

See page 92 to learn more.

EXCEPTIONAL DIMENSION #5
Courage

The key is taking chances and proceeding with them despite the obstacles that lie ahead!

See page 96 to learn more.

EXCEPTIONAL DIMENSION #6
Innovation

The key is to be creative and use a synergistic approach to develop new ideas that are impactful and satisfy needs of the market!

See page 99 to learn more.

The Exceptional Dimensions

EXCEPTIONAL DIMENSION #7
Hard working

The key is keeping your foot on the gas so your competitor does not move in!

See page 102 to learn more.

EXCEPTIONAL DIMENSION #8
Resilience

The key is to bounce back quickly from derailments and major disruptions!

See page 105 to learn more.

EXCEPTIONAL DIMENSION #9
Delegation

The key is to make the best use of your time and skills and to help other people develop to their full potential!

See page 110 to learn more.

EXCEPTIONAL DIMENSION #10
Perseverance

The key is to identify enemies of perseverance and work to defeat them. You will be able to rise above to accomplish your loftiest goals!

See page 117 to learn more.

EXCEPTIONAL DIMENSION #11
Passion

The key is to follow your heart, but check it with your head!

See page 121 to learn more.

EXCEPTIONAL DIMENSION #12
Positive Attitude

The key is to eliminate any negative mind talk and just do it!

See page 124 to learn more.

Eddie's Life

The life of Eddie Crouch began on December 4, 1933 in Sugarcreek, Missouri, a small town located just outside of Independence and not far from the home of Harry Truman. Eddie was born in his family home, not in a hospital, which was common in those days. Eddie's parents, Lillian and Wallace, were extremely proud of their home. It was the first home that they bought when they married and it still stands there today. Eddie was the third born in the Crouch family.

Eddie's sister, Marguerite, is six years older than Eddie. Eddie's brother, Wallace Crouch Jr. is four years older than Eddie. Eddie also had a little sister, Billy Rose, who unfortunately succumbed to an accident and died at an early age. Eddie was only three or four years old when the accident happened but he remembers certain life events about his younger sister. For example, he remembers his older sister giving bicycle rides to Billy Rose more frequently than him! This wasn't fair! Or one time when they were playing around, Billy Rose accidently got her eye poked with a broom hook. She was a fun-loving and playful child that everyone enjoyed.

Eddie vividly remembers Billy Rose's funeral, which had a lasting impression on him.

Eddie's parents moved to Kansas City, Missouri, before school started. Eddie's dad worked right across the street in a grocery store. He was a meat cutter in the grocery store. Eddie was four years old at the time and therefore was not in school yet. So he spent a lot of time at the store. One of his jobs was to take the 50-pound gunny-bags of potatoes and put them into 10-pound paper sacks for customers to purchase. By the way, for those who know Kansas City history, this was the old Kaminski store on Sterling Street.

Eddie attended the Seventh-day Adventist Church School, the Kansas City Junior Academy, which had 10 grades in the school. Eddie started in 1st grade. Grades 1-4 were all conducted in one classroom. The same teacher taught all those grades and there were about 25 students in the room. Eddie's brother and sister also attended the same school and took Eddie to school every day on a bus and a streetcar. It was about a 30-minute streetcar ride to school. Eddie was in this school through the 10th grade, which in today's terminology would have been through junior high.

After the 4th grade, Eddie moved into another classroom and stayed there through the 8th grade. The 9th and 10th grades were in another room. Throughout Eddie's time at the Academy, he rode back and forth on the streetcar with kids from the public schools. He got to know many of the kids in the neighborhood who went to public school because of riding the same streetcar and buses. As typically can happen, Eddie and some of the kids got scuffling and playing around on the streetcar. One day, while they were playing around, one of the students had a pencil in her notebook and it inadvertently went right into Eddie's hand. The lead point is still in his hand today, a reminder of from where he came, and how far he has come. Another memory from his school days was the fact that Eddie was tall, probably the tallest boy in the class. It didn't take him too long to realize his commanding presence was an advantage, one that stayed with him as a leader later in life.

Eddie also remembers that he was an average student who got average grades because he really didn't apply himself to his studies. The students were obviously very close and stayed in touch with each other after school via telephone or would play together in the neighborhood. Occasionally, Eddie would stay around and play with his classmates before heading home.

Eddie's mom and dad had to work hard for him to attend the Academy and keep him there. Eddie's mom was religious and felt that attending a church school was important. Eddie's dad, although not overly religious, was an extremely hard worker and worked throughout World War II six days a week as a meat cutter with Kroger Meats. When Eddie was 12 or 13 years old his father was able to get him a job in a Kroger store stocking shelves. After the war, Eddie's dad opened a small butcher shop in Kansas City, Missouri. This was the first time that Eddie saw his dad working for himself and not for someone else. Eddie was about 13 years old at this time and he often visited his father at the store almost every Saturday. Eddie not only enjoyed being with his father, but also learning from him.

Eddie was a little younger than his brother and sister. Since they were closer together in age, they naturally spent much more time together than with Eddie. While Eddie had a good relationship with his brother and sister, they did not "hang out" together.

Most of Eddie's friends at school were in the 10th grade while he was in the 9th grade. So when they finished the 10th grade, most of them moved on to school at the Sunnydale Academy, a boarding school in Centralia, in central Missouri. This school was a four-year high school (grades 9, 10, 11, 12). Eddie talked to his parents about moving on to Sunnydale with his classmates. He could complete his 10th grade there. This would be an expensive move because it was a boarding school. But Eddie talked to the school principal as well as others who were familiar with the school and they agreed that if he worked during the summer in the area, that money could go toward his school tuition. It also meant that Eddie would work during the school year after classes. Eddie worked on a farm and in the dairy. This was difficult because it was hard to focus on schoolwork when he was so tired from his demanding work schedule. But he was responsible to his duties and knew he needed to *work hard* to make this happen.

Sunnydale had about 150 students, and Eddie had a very positive experience at Sunnydale. His roommate was one of his best friends from Kansas City.

When Eddie went to Sunnydale it was difficult for him to see his family as often as he wanted. This was a real challenge since Eddie was always in a close-knit family environment. Since he was working during the summer and after school each day, he would hitchhike home on a weekend or during a vacation several times a year. His mom and dad would come to visit him every few weeks, driving down from Kansas City to Centralia.

Unfortunately, the war interrupted the education of Eddie's brother and sister. The workforce was depleted so they left school (never graduating) and joined the workforce. For most of her life, Eddie's mom was "at-home" keeping the family going, especially to church! But during the war she too went to work and got a job at the Kroger Warehouse.

After Eddie graduated from high school (Eddie was 18), he went to work at the Sambol meatpacking plant. The plant was strictly beef packing (no other types of meat) and Eddie learned the entire process that went on in that plant, including boning the meat, selling the meat, and delivering the meat.

This early understanding of the entire meat processing

procedure laid a deep foundation that later translated into Eddie's *passion* for this industry, and it also paved the way for the application of this business principle into all his other businesses.

Eddie married and started a family. He had 2 children and already had built a strong commitment to his family life.

While working at the meat packing company, Eddie met and became friends with John Fenton. Eddie had met John's sister, Patsy, when he had an opportunity to work on her car. Eddie wanted to remove part of her engine (four barrel carburetor) and install it in his car, since the cars were alike. Eddie also would give her some money for those parts.

As Eddie was working on her car, Patsy heard that making this switch of carburetors was not a good deal for her. So she called Eddie and said she wanted her carburetors back but Eddie had already completed the job.

Sadly, about a year later Eddie lost his wife in a car accident. After the death of his wife, and for several years thereafter, John would have Eddie over to his house periodically to have dinner. At one of these occasions Eddie asked John to invite his sister Patsy to join them, which he did. Eddie and Patsy would drive over to John's house in her car for dinner. After dinner, he took her home and gave her a good night kiss. Eddie stole Patsy's heart that night and they were married on December 24, 1959. Eddie's family continued to grow. Eddie and Patsy had two children together and they are blessed to currently have nine grandchildren.

Eddie was learning the meat business from the inside out! What he now needed was to grasp all the important aspects of the "outside"… the customer side. The most influential person in this regard was his dad. Eddie saw him work for years at Kroger and then start his own business in his shop at the city market. Eddie saw his father in his shop cutting meat and dealing with his customers and suppliers. He was always well liked by his customers. He had that kind of personality. He was a good talker as well as a good listener. He knew everyone by his or her first name, and was very personable in how he greeted him or her. Eddie was truly inspired just by watching his father work with people.

EXCEPTIONAL DIMENSION #1
Building Relationships

The key is to listen first and then deliver on what you heard!

See page 76 to learn more.

A few memories about Eddie's father's meat shop; he was in the meat shop for about 6 to 8 months before a business opportunity opened up at the Oscar Mayer Meat distributorship. His dad purchased the route. He closed his meat shop and took on the distributorship since it really meant more money. Now Eddie's dad had about 30 to 35 customers that he called on every other day. He ran this meat route for four or five years.

When Eddie came home from school, he would ride with his father on the Oscar Mayer meat route. This really interested Eddie. His dad would go from store to store upon his meat route and would fill his orders right out of his truck. He and his dad talked about the demand from these small "mom and pop" neighborhood stores. These small shops could not individually order in large quantities and therefore paid more for their meat. It was obvious to Eddie that these small shops were struggling. So he told his dad that once he gets out of school he might be interested in putting together his own route with just the small shops. Eddie was about 18 years old at the time.

He talked with his dad about becoming a meat cutter and asked him to introduce him to his customers on his route. His dad backed him up and told his customers what Eddie intended to do. Eddie went out and bought himself a van. Every morning Eddie would call all of his customers and take their order for meat. Then he would call the packinghouses with his combined orders and have them ready for pickup. He would then deliver the meat to his customers. He used this process for about 4 to 5 months and still wasn't making the kind of money he felt he needed to support his wife and growing family. Eddie got to know all the key people at all the packinghouses and got along very well with all of them. One of the meat packing houses, Sambol, approached him about finding someone to work in the packinghouse. Eddie offered himself for the job and when asked when he could start, he told them he could start the next day. Eddie worked at the Sambol Meat Packing Company for 13 years.

Here's where we are now; Eddie has had a hands-on education in the meat industry. He has seen and understands the importance of the customer relationships. He has had a chance to assess a business opportunity and developed his personal network. It was time to move on and he had a vision.

> **EXCEPTIONAL DIMENSION #2**
> **Visionary**
>
> *The key is to create a picture of what success looks like and then build a plan to achieve it!*
>
> See page 80 to learn more.

The Early Business Years

One of Eddie's first ventures into business ownership was a filling station (gas station). He ran that about a year. John Fenton his friend and business partner was very enthused about the venture. However, it was not successful. It wasn't a failure either. It was a great learning experience. As Eddie recalls, "Many of the people in the neighborhood didn't have automobiles or didn't have the money to buy gas even though at that time, gasoline was $.19 a gallon." Eddie's station pumped up to 2,500 gallons per month but his margin was only three cents a gallon gross. And while he did have some inside service work (he had a full-time mechanic), it still did not generate enough money he felt he needed. It just was not where he wanted to be from a financial standpoint. Eddie actually made more money at Sambol than he did in the filling station. So money was important at this stage of his life. He went back to the Sambol meat packing plant. Then he sold the gas station. "I guess the lesson here was knowing your market potential and location selection", said Eddie.

Eddie was about 27 years old when he went back to his previous job at Sambol. The most difficult part of the job was the physical side. The best and easiest part of the job was the Wednesday delivery of the packaged lunchmeat to the customers because it expanded his interaction with customers and it helped to solidify relationships. He stayed with Sambol until 1965.

It was at this time that a friend in the meat distribution business (route delivery), Brownie, died of a heart attack. Brownie had an Oscar Mayer distributorship, similar to the one that Eddie's father had. Brownie's widow had no training in or knowledge about running the business. All she had was his route book that listed all this customers (no addresses) and what they ordered. Because the customers needed product on a regular basis, she would lose the route to another distributor. Mrs. Brown would have gotten nothing out of her husband's route business.

"Before the route was handed over to another distributor, I offered to buy the business for $5,000 from Mrs. Brown. It was a win-win, for her and for me!" Eddie related. She thankfully accepted! His goal was to retain every customer. Eddie visited each customer, told them about Brownie's death and that he was going to take over the route and continue to provide the service. There was 100% participation! There were all types of customers on the route from large chain stores to small mom-and-pop stores. Eddie knew some of the customers from his days at Sambol and about 20% of the customers knew Eddie.

> **EXCEPTIONAL DIMENSION #3**
> **Communication**
>
> *The key is consistency, impact, and clarity: consider what, who, when, where, and how your communications will be delivered most effectively!*
>
> See page 85 to learn more.

Eddie had ended up with about 60 to 65 customers that he delivered product to per week (different route each day of the week). At the same time, he called on other accounts that he didn't have and tried to sell his product to these customers as well. He gradually built his business from these prospects as well.

Eddie sold his products and explained to the customer that he would be there each week at the same time with the product that the customer needed. Eddie would not just deliver the meat; he would unpack it, stamp it, and put it in the case. In other words, he merchandised the product for his customers. This value added approach enhanced Eddie's ability to gain new accounts and retain the old ones. Eddie worked this distributorship for 5 years.

Eddie was now 37 years old.

At this time, the rumor on the street was that Oscar Mayer was going to eliminate all its routes and move all products to large warehouses that would directly serve the customers, providing everything needed for the stores. Therefore, Eddie knew he had to sell his route before Oscar Mayer would just take it over. Eventually, one of his customers was interested in the route and purchased it from Eddie. He had approached Eddie with a desire to have an opportunity to own a route and Eddie was ready to sell his route. The new owner was aware of the Oscar Mayer strategy and knew the transition would take time. It came together for both parties! "Another win-win" said Eddie.

> **EXCEPTIONAL DIMENSION #4**
> **Decision-making**
>
> *The key is to make your decision sound and do it rapidly!*
>
> See page 92 to learn more.

With the proceeds for the sale, he purchased his own meat company called Mission Meats in Mission, Kansas. Eddie included his brother, Walter, as part owner of the new meat company, although he made no financial investment in the company. Mission Meats sold their products to restaurants in the Kansas City area.

The restaurant business was different in that you called daily to determine their needs. Patsy, Eddie's wife, and Jean, Wallace's wife, plus some other office staff would call the restaurants every day to determine the types of meat cuts the restaurant required. Patsy was involved in many different aspects of the meat company, both in the office and in the plant. Eddie was running Mission Meats for about a year. He found that his brother was more conservative and wasn't looking to grow and branch out further like Eddie was thinking. After negotiating several options,

Eddie offered his brother an opportunity to buy him out and own the whole company. His brother took it. So for a period of about 6 months, Eddie was out of the meat business but looking for new, exciting, and profitable opportunities to feed his passions. He and Patsy lived off the proceeds of his brother's buyout. Eddie began to look around for another business opportunity as well as building relationships with several banks for future financing.

EXCEPTIONAL DIMENSION #5
Courage

The key is taking chances and proceeding with them despite the obstacles that lie ahead!

See page 96 to learn more.

Eddie found a facility at 47th and Mission. It was a small business where we could set up the Crouch Meat Company. Eddie established an opening date and he and Patsy went out to talk to future customers about supplying them with meat.

A key decision here was that Eddie decided to specialize in ground beef! This was his key differentiation. He marketed his product by simply stating that the Crouch Meat was *"Famous For It's Ground Beef"* – an advertising tagline that proved successful!

EXCEPTIONAL DIMENSION #6
Innovation

The key is to be creative and use a synergistic approach to develop new ideas that are impactful and satisfy needs of the market!

See page 99 to learn more.

He did not want to be in direct competition with his brother and experience told him that he did not want to get involved in all the various cuts of meat. He wanted to keep it simple and be the best! Ground beef was the answer and now his specialty. He called on big companies that ran hamburger restaurants as well as hamburger stands. He wanted his product in all them and to become the top ground beef provider. He achieved that in the Kansas City area.

Eddie started the Crouch Meat Company in 1972 with one truck, and three employees, himself, Patsy and his son, Mike. The three of them worked from early morning until late at night every day in their new business. They added an employee after about six months but still kept up this work pace for about two years. It was their life and their passion!

> **EXCEPTIONAL DIMENSION #7**
> **Hard working**
>
> *The key is keeping your foot on the gas so your competitor does not move in!*
>
> See page 102 to learn more.

Eddie had a vision and he wanted to grow the business. In order to quickly learn more about the meat processing business, Eddie attended seminars, conventions, and conferences for the industry. He learned about the latest equipment available and saw what he needed to produce more meat as he grew. He also met people in the meat packing business that he saw would potentially become his suppliers.

> **EXCEPTIONAL DIMENSION #2**
> **Visionary**
>
> *The key is to create a picture of what success looks like and then build a plan to achieve it!*
>
> See page 80 to learn more.

Locally, the Restaurant Association would stage trade shows. Patsy and Eddie would set up a booth and cook hamburgers for the attendees. Naturally, their booth was one of the most popular and word quickly spread about Crouch Meat's fabulous hamburgers. All good advertising for attracting new business!

In his second year of operation, Eddie was approached by the labor union. This could have become a real challenge to his start-up operation. They wanted to organize the company and indicated that several of his employees had signed up for Union representation. Eddie had about 15 employees at this time.

The local Union president came into Eddie's office and stated his case. Eddie said "No, thank you!" and ended the conversation. Several of the employees and Union reps picketed the company and the employees went on strike. Eddie, Patsy, their son, Mike, and several others were brought in to keep the plant going.

EXCEPTION DIMENSION #8
Resilience

The key is to bounce back quickly from derailments and major disruptions!

See page 105 to learn more.

The next morning, Eddie found that the tires of some of his trucks had been slashed. But he stayed the course and did not accept the Union's offer. And in a matter of days, the Union withdrew. Eddie hired all his workers back, including those who walked the picket line.

Eddie purchased his meat from the packing companies like Sambol with whom he still had a great relationship. Eddie had been at all the packinghouses and knew the in's and out's of each. Therefore, he could shop for the best quality at the best price. Patsy, who had sales experience, had never sold meat before. Eddie told her she was going to learn. So, she did!

EXCEPTION DIMENSION #9
Delegation

The key is to make the best use of your time and skills and to help other people develop to their full potential!

See page 110 to learn more.

Patsy sold Crouch Meat products to the Gilbert Robinson restaurants. Initially, she got off to a rather rocky start when the Gilbert Robinson's purchasing agent was hesitant to do business with a company like Crouch Meat that was not even in the Yellow Pages! In fact, even though Crouch Meat had product in one the Robinson operations, the purchasing agent told her to stop selling to the other locations. One afternoon, that restaurant location called in a panic and asked if Crouch Meat could deliver product to their restaurant by the next morning. The order they had received from another meat company was bad and they needed meat products as soon as possible. Because of being told not to deliver meat to them, Patsy promised that Couch Meat would have the meat ready as long as the customer would come and pick it up. He agreed and picked up the order at Crouch Meat. The "crisis" was averted!

The next day Patsy got a call from the purchasing agent and he requested that she come in right away to his office. Patsy was shaking in her boots outside of his office door. He communicated to Patsy that their vice president had tasted the Crouch Meat product the previous night and deemed it the best he had ever tasted and that he wanted Crouch Meat to supply them product. Crouch Meat would now deliver product to half of their stores, and if they did a good job, they would get all of their stores. At that time, Gilbert Robinson had about 14 restaurants and Patsy had several weeks to prove they could handle one half their restaurants. If the product

> **EXCEPTIONAL DIMENSION #10**
> **Perseverance**
>
> *The key is to identify enemies of perseverance and work to defeat them. You will be able to rise above to accomplish your loftiest goals!*
>
> See page 117 to learn more.

and service were unsatisfactory, she would lose them all; if it were satisfactory she get them all. With hard work and perseverance, Crouch Meat gained all the stores and Gilbert Robinson became Crouch Meat's largest account, driving much of the company's early success.

About this time the President Nixon Administration put a freeze on all meat prices. No one could raise the price of meat. So the packinghouses virtually shut down because they could not sell their meat at the frozen price and survive.

Naturally, Gilbert Robinson called Patsy and asked "Are you going to be able to serve all of our needs during this price freeze?" She looked over at Eddie who nodded his head and she said, yes, we could do that. Because the packinghouses were not able to sell their meat at the prices of the freeze, Eddie went out and bought his own cattle! There was no violation of the freeze because Eddie paid the farmer to kill the cattle and deliver the cattle to his meat company. Since they were his cattle, he didn't break the law or violate the freeze rules.

> **EXCEPTIONAL DIMENSION #6**
> **Innovation**
>
> *The key is to be creative and use a synergistic approach to develop new ideas that are impactful and satisfy needs of the market!*
>
> See page 99 to learn more.

Not only was Crouch Meat able to fill the needs of the Gilbert Robinson restaurants in Kansas City, they also began to supply meat around the country to the other Gilbert Robinson locations, i.e. St. Louis, New Orleans and others. None of the other meat suppliers could deliver because the packinghouses were down all over the country. This demand increased and lasted 3 to 6 months. More people were lined up at Crouch Meat's door to get supplied. The Sambol connection was very valuable during this time because they knew where Eddie could purchase cattle directly. This was a big surge in the Crouch Meat Company and they doubled their business in this six-month period.

One restaurant, Harry Starker's on the Kansas City Plaza, did the same thing as Eddie, buying their meet directly. The difference was that Starker's had no use for the meat trimmings. They were just interested in the fillets, steaks, etc. So Eddie bought all of his trimmings to put into his specialty ground beef.

By this time Crouch Meat had 90% of the hamburger business in Kansas City! The exception was McDonald's, which was supplied by another. Crouch Meat now had between 100 in 150 accounts.

This was an exciting time for Eddie and Patsy. They developed a passion for the business, their business had grown; they experienced success, and were fast becoming the premier supplier in the area. But it was only the beginning.

> **EXCEPTIONAL DIMENSION #11**
> **Passion**
>
> *The key is to follow your heart, but check it with your head!*
>
> See page 121 to learn more.

Enter Wendy's

About this time, two gentlemen arrived at the Crouch Meat Company indicating that they were about to bring a new hamburger franchise to Kansas City. It was named Wendy's. Eddie gave them a sample 5-pound box of his ground beef. About a month later, Patsy received a phone call from Wendy's for an order of 400 pounds of ground beef. They never said that Eddie would get their business; they just called up and placed an order. 400 pounds of ground beef is a lot of ground beef and since they made quarter pound hamburgers, the order represented 1,600 hamburger patties. The very next day they called up and placed another order for the same size. At this time, Wendy's had opened only one restaurant in downtown Kansas City. They continued to do this for eight or nine months until they opened their second restaurant! As a result, business continued to grow for Crouch Meat Company. And remember, Crouch Meat Company also supplied 90% of the other hamburger stands in the greater Kansas City area including Burger King.

Wendy's grew rapidly and put up another dozen restaurants within the next 18 months. And for the Crouch Meat Company, this practically doubled their business. Frankly, they did not have the room in their small meat plant for this volume. At this point Eddie got extremely interested in Wendy's and learned that they were growing all over the country. They were buying locally in Kansas,

> **EXCEPTIONAL DIMENSION #5**
> **Courage**
>
> *The key is taking chances and proceeding with them despite the obstacles that lie ahead!*
>
> See page 96 to learn more.

in Wichita and Topeka, up in Iowa in Des Moines and down to Springfield, Missouri. So Patsy and Eddie jumped on a plane and went to the Wendy's headquarters in Columbus, Ohio. They presented a plan whereby they could handle all these locations if they could become the sole distributor for Wendy's. Although no contract was signed, they said okay!

Eddie Crouch, David Thomas, John Hamra, Don George

Eddie and Patsy began to fill orders all over the Midwest. They had to buy additional tractor-trailer trucks to meet the demand they had from Des Moines to St. Louis. Plus, the agreement meant that they could no longer sell to other accounts, only distributing to Wendy's. They had to drop all their other accounts. This was difficult as these were all of their longtime and loyal customers!

Eddie also needed to expand his line of credit since he had to use upfront money, and was paid by Wendy's only after he delivered the product. Eddie was able to secure a two and a half million-dollar line of credit in order to purchase meat, process it into patties, and deliver product in a 15-state area. On their trip to Columbus, Patsy and Eddie visited a local plant that supplied Wendy's in that area and learned the procedure that Wendy's wanted to be installed in their supplier's facilities. Basically, it meant new equipment and new procedures in order to meet the product standards and demands of Wendy's. For example, Wendy's wanted two 20-pound bags of product in a milk carton size container to be used to deliver to the various stores. Each Wendy's restaurant received the ground beef and the restaurant had a small patty machine to convert the ground beef into a hamburger patty. Crouch Meat had to make a delivery to every store in their region every third day. Eddie had to set up and purchase all his equipment, get everything up and running, and Wendy's would come in and inspect their process before any agreement was reached.

However, they had a binding verbal contract to begin manufacturing ground beef for the Wendy's patties for the restaurants in that region. At no time did Eddie think that he wasn't going to get

> **EXCEPTIONAL DIMENSION #12**
> **Positive Attitude**
>
> *The key is to eliminate any negative mind talk and just do it!*
>
> See page 124 to learn more.

the contract or that he couldn't fulfill Wendy's standards. He would do whatever it took.

Eddie used excess meat trimmings from meat packinghouses to put more fat into his hamburgers to meet Wendy's standards. The standard was 74% lean and 26% fat and Eddie was able to meet that standard on a consistent basis by applying and mixing in meat trimmings. Eddie continued to purchase his meat trimmings from Harry Starker's who didn't use the trimmings in their restaurant and meats.

Crouch Meat Company's business was now expanding into all of Kansas, Missouri, and Iowa and business was growing by leaps and bounds because all the Wendy's restaurants bought high quantities of meat. Before any business was finalized with Wendy's, they wanted to be sure that he could handle the three states. This expansion meant that Eddie had to get more equipment and increase his transportation capabilities. Eddie received notice that a packinghouse was going on the auction block in St. Joseph, Missouri. It was a large meatpacking house. The equipment being auctioned met Eddie's needs, including eight tractor-trailers. This was exactly what Eddie was looking for to handle delivery for Wendy's stores in his region. In order to bid on any of the equipment he had to have a letter of credit from the bank. Eddie would need a $400,000 letter of credit for the entire package or a $200,000 line of credit for bidding on just the equipment. When he went to the bank, he asked for a letter of credit for the auction and the bank gave them the entire $400,000 line of credit. Eddie's line of credit came from the Morgan bank in Kansas City, the same bank that supported the Wendy's franchises in Kansas City. The bank tied the financing or letter of credit to Eddie's accounts receivable and since they were already financially supporting the Wendy's franchise, they were able to see the potential in Eddie's request for a letter of credit.

EXCEPTIONAL DIMENSION #4
Decision-making

The key is to make your decision sound and do it rapidly!

See page 92 to learn more.

This was the largest transaction opportunity that Eddie had up to this point in his business career. So Eddie and Jack Wylie, his close friend, went to St. Joseph. The auction began with bidding on the piece parts of the plant's equipment. However, you could bid on the entire package. There were only three or four people who had the full line of credit, including Eddie that could do so. Jack encouraged Eddie to bid on the entire package. Eddie told Jack that he didn't want the entire plant but Jack told him that he would support it as a full partner and put in half of whatever the final bid was. The others dropped out and Eddie ended up with the winning bid for the entire package!

At the same time the local press from St. Joseph's was there and they swamped Eddie with questions regarding his potential ownership of the plant. There was keen interest because of the employment needed in St. Joseph and the press knew of Eddie's business with Wendy's. Now, because of the piecemeal part of the auction the process meant that if the piece parts totaled more money than Eddie's bid for the entire plant the piece parts would go to those bidders. But no one knew that until the end of the auction when they could total up all the piece parts. The auction started the bidding and the trucks were the first component. Eddie recalls, "I was tied up with the press and wasn't even able to bid on what I had originally come to acquire!"

This entire auction process took the full day. There was a large quantity of equipment to be auctioned off in addition to the eight tractor-trailers and again, hence he wouldn't know whether he got the entire package until all the bidding was complete. In other words, if the equipment bids were more than the package bids, then the results would be split with those bidding on the equipment. Those bidding on the entire package would get all the buildings and anything else that was still available.

In the end, Eddie won all the buildings and the land and all the coolers and equipment that weren't auctioned off in the piece part section. Jack Wylie called the bank in Chicago that originally owned the meatpacking plant and they agreed to finance Eddie and Jack for the purchase of the entire plant. What started out as wanting a few trucks turned into owning an entire plant!

This particular facility was much larger than Eddie's North Kansas City plant. But he did not want to close his North Kansas City plant because of its central location. At the same time he learned that the government, in order to keep prices to the farmer at a certain level, have been buying cheese and storing it in railroad cars all over the country. Although the railroad cars were refrigerated the government had no place to unload and store the cheese for future distribution. Eddie had an idea and decided to visit the Government Services Administration (the GSA) offices in Kansas City. He went to the government offices without an appointment and asked to speak with whomever was in charge of the government cheese program. When they met, he told them that he had a refrigerated facility that could handle the government cheese. They immediately asked Eddie how soon he could get his facility up and running. Eddie went back to his newly acquired plant to determine how quickly he could have it ready to accept the cheese. They had it cooling down in a matter of a couple of days. When he informed the government they said they would begin shipping the cheese in right away.

EXCEPTIONAL DIMENSION #6
Innovation

The key is to be creative and use a synergistic approach to develop new ideas that are impactful and satisfy needs of the market!

See page 99 to learn more.

The cheese would be delivered by rail and the railroad tracks at Eddie's facility hadn't been used in years. Once these railcars started to arrive, the tracks were unable to bear the weight. Eddie called the railroad company to see if he could get them to reinforce the track. He was informed that they no longer own that rail line; it belonged to another railroad company that was currently in bankruptcy. Eddie talked with the bankruptcy court in Chicago and asked for a solution. He was informed that the best they could do was sell Eddie the railroad track. The track was several miles long and the court would not repair it, only sell it. So in true *exceptional entrepreneur* style, Eddie bought it!

Eddie called the railroad company in St. Joseph's to come out and repair the track and they did it on a contract basis. The repair took several weeks. Eddie had to unload the cars that were there in order to get the track cleared for the next load to be

---

EXCEPTIONAL DIMENSION #5
Courage

The key is taking chances and proceeding with them despite the obstacles that lie ahead!

See page 96 to learn more.

---

delivered. Railroad cars began rolling in and eventually Eddie had stored about 25,000,000 pounds of cheese in his refrigerated area of his meat plant with a staff of eight people. Once this process started Eddie received a check every month from the government for storing the cheese. Eddie was now in the cold storage cheese business for the federal government.

In the meantime, the Wendy's operation continued and Eddie divided his time between the North Kansas City plant and his new facility in St. Joseph. The cheese business lasted about nine months. Eddie had purchased five used tractor-trailers to be able to fulfill his contract of supplying Wendy's in the three-state region. Wendy's sent in Terry Calloway from their headquarters in Ohio. Terry helped Eddie expand his Wendy's territories into Oklahoma, Tennessee, and the other contiguous states.

Wendy's also expanded the product line they wanted Eddie to deliver in addition to the hamburger meat. Eddie would handle all the dairy products that went into all the Wendy's stores in this expanded region. This included the Frosty product as well as all the produce for the stores. Essentially, Eddie began to supply everything that went into a Wendy's store in his region except the paper goods. This immediately doubled his business. By the way, Eddie purchased all the produce he needed (lettuce, tomatoes etc.) from local Kansas City produce companies. The entire ice cream product for the Frosty came from John Dorsey and his St. Louis company.

Wendy's management inspected and approved all of the sources that Eddie used. Once Eddie had his pickup and delivery processes in place and he performed so well for Wendy's in his region, they expanded his territory into Colorado and the Western states. That prompted Eddie to go to Colorado and start another meat processing facility. Eddie started to serve the markets out of the Denver facility and maintained his Midwestern region. He now delivered to all the Wendy's and all their products in 15 states! The outcome of this growth in business was the wealth

Eddie created as well as the jobs not only at his meatpacking plant, but also for all the people associated to the delivery of produce and ice cream to serve the entire area.

Eddie hired Terry Galloway away from Wendy's to run his Denver plant. Eddie started producing and delivering Wendy's products. Within three months he received the agreement from Wendy's to handle that new territory out of Denver. He started with a small facility but after a year, purchased a larger plant about the size of his Kansas City facility. The Denver plant was equipped to process meat. Eddie sent his plant manager and his daughter, Terry, and her husband to Denver to run the operations side of the plant. His daughter ran the Cryovac® section of the plant. This happened in 1981. By this time, Eddie had 44 employees in Kansas City and 25 in the Denver plant. Crouch Meat was servicing 284 stores in 14 states.

EXCEPTIONAL DIMENSION #9
Delegation

The key is to make the best use of your time and skills and to help other people develop to their full potential!

See page 110 to learn more.

Grand Opening 1983 Lenexa Meatpacking Plant

The Wendy's account started in 1974. By 1983, Eddie's plants were processing and delivering 1,200,000 lbs. of meat every week. Wendy's estimated that equated to 5,200,000 hamburgers!

Anytime Eddie opened a new territory, he visited the customers. He met the store managers, the franchise owners and the employees that he would be servicing. He'd ask these people if they were satisfied with what he was doing and was there anything else he could do for them. Perhaps they would want some changes made and what might they be? The idea was to make the customers happy.

> **EXCEPTIONAL DIMENSION #1**
> **Building Relationships**
>
> *The key is to listen first and then deliver on what you heard!*
>
> See page 76 to learn more.

Eddie was going full bore in his Wendy's business when Jack Wylie, his original partner, came to him and asked if he could buy him out. Eddie did not want to get out of the business. Jack offered to buy one of the two plants, Kansas City or Denver. Jack made an offer for the Kansas City plant. Eddie would keep the Denver plant. The arrangement was on an annuity basis whereby income was generated on a monthly basis. This income lasted several years! Another win-win for both parties!

> **EXCEPTIONAL DIMENSION #4**
> **Decision-making**
>
> *The key is to make your decision sound and do it rapidly!*
>
> See page 92 to learn more.

Everything ran smoothly out of the Denver plant until one of Eddie's suppliers ran into trouble. This same supplier supplied the government with meat. It was publicized that this company had sold tainted meat to the government and it mentioned that they sold meat to a Wendy's supplier, which of course was Crouch Meat. This packinghouse fought the government's claim for reimbursement of several million dollars worth of meat. The government in turn brought charges against the packinghouse and put the owner in jail.

Eddie's plant ran daily tests on his meat in a lab and sent those reports to Wendy's. This was what Wendy's required to insure quality was maintained. This was a standard operating procedure and was in place well before the government's publicized fight with their meatpacking supplier. "All of a sudden" Eddie recalls, "I received notice that Wendy's was pulling our distributorship away, even though my meat always exceeded Wendy's standards." Eddie had no choice, but to take their products and turn them over to Wendy's new distributor. Eddie shut the door on the Denver plant!

Meanwhile, Eddie and Patsy sold their home, moved their furniture into storage of one of his trucks, and moved into a trailer.

Eddie knew that all his products were perfect and had the test results from the labs on a daily basis to prove it. Eddie sued Wendy's and the suit was settled in Eddie's favor. Eddie eventually recovered his money from the new distributor for the remaining product and sold his plant in Denver. Eddie was now out of the meat business in 1984.

> **EXCEPTIONAL DIMENSION #12**
> **Positive Attitude**
>
> *The key is to eliminate any negative mind talk and just do it!*
>
> See page 124 to learn more.

This setback could have derailed Eddie's business career! Yet the *Exceptional Entrepreneur* saw this only as a pause.

Life After Wendy's
The Journey Continues

After the close down, Eddie's family wondered and asked what's next? Are we going to continue to work for you? Are you going to get into something else? What?

EXCEPTIONAL DIMENSION #8
Resilience

The key is to bounce back quickly from derailments and major disruptions!

See page 105 to learn more.

Eddie had always thought about the convenience store business. Ever since Eddie had the Oscar Mayer route and had seen the profitability of convenience stores where he supplied meat, he had thought about someday opening up a convenience store.

So in 1985, Eddie started to investigate companies like 7-Eleven and Circle K. He talked to some of their people and became very interested in the business. He thought about his family, he had money to invest, and he decided to get into the convenience store business where they all could work.

He selected the property at K7 Highway and Johnson Drive (now commonly known as Crouch Corner). The project started with a convenience store that had a dry cleaner, gas station, carwash, and fast food, much like today's QuikTrip stores. Eddie wanted an outstanding convenience store so he invested in the appearance of the store. He even included eating space inside. This turned out to be a mistake. In a sense, Eddie overbuilt his first convenience store. It cost Eddie too much, which made it difficult to retire the debt on this facility. The income the store generated was not sufficient to cover the debt.

A year and a half later he started another store in Edwardsville. He learned from the first store not to overbuild. "I was very cautious regarding my investment in building the second store," he recalls. For example, the size was smaller then his first store, no carwash was included, and there was no other business inside the store other than food. This store was a profitable store! No more than 6 months later the 2 other stores quickly followed.

Eddie ended up building a total of four stores (the Crouch C Stores). Eddie states, "One word of advice is not to put all of the stores under one name. Instead, each should have carried its own separate books. If you have several locations, make each one a separate business." That way, as in Eddie's case, the unprofitable store or location doesn't pull down the other profitable stores or locations. Eddie could have retained the profitable stores and closed the two that weren't so profitable. Going forward he kept each location a separate entity. Providing more flexibility from a financial perspective is key in being able to close or bankrupt one while retaining the others.

Eddie had the convenience store business from 1985 to 1990. During those five years, Matt, his son, ran the first, third and fourth stores, while Candy Merrick ran the second store. Matt functioned as the general manager over those stores and had individual store managers in each location.

Eddie just couldn't stay away from the meat business so in 1988 he bought a beef boning and packinghouse. Eddie bought whole sides of beef, boned them, packed them in Cryon packages, and sold those to grocery stores. This is where Eddie devoted most of his time and energy while Matt and Candy took care of the four stores.

During this timeframe Eddie's son, Patrick, came to him and asked for his support for a friend who was working in the trucking business in Omaha, Nebraska. The owner was thinking of closing the business and Patrick's friend wanted to know if Eddie would take over the running of that business. Eddie bought the business and assumed the role of an absentee owner, which is never a good idea. (You must be there in order to manage the business.) In this case, Eddie learned that one employee was stealing from his company. Eddie eventually closed this business but he now had the equipment and trucks.

One of the key synergies between this trucking business and the convenience stores was using the convenience store gas service to fill its trucks. This gave stability to the cash flow of the stores. However, when Eddie had to close the trucking business, the convenience store lost a sizable portion of their operating cash flow. Unfortunately, Eddie had to declare bankruptcy on all four stores, even though the second store had already been paid for and the debt totally retired on that store.

So now he was able to jump into the "piggyback" business, where a truck and trailer would come together after the trailer was delivered via rail.

> **EXCEPTIONAL DIMENSION #8**
> **Resilience**
>
> *The key is to bounce back quickly from derailments and major disruptions!*
>
> See page 105 to learn more.

Patsy went to a trucking convention in Atlanta and attracted businesses for Eddie's piggyback service. Eddie worked out of the boning plant and had about a dozen tractor-trailers for his piggyback service. This piggyback business and the boning plant all lasted until 1990.

While he was still ahead financially, Eddie closed the doors on the boning plant when meat became scarce and it was no longer profitable to run.

In the meantime, another opportunity surfaced. Eddie's insurance agent, Larry Spencer, who covered his convenience stores, came to him with a unique proposal. The Federal Communications Commission (FCC) was carefully watching the growth of the wireless industry and specifically, watching the growth of the major companies in the wireless business. So far, ATT, Verizon, Sprint, and T-Mobile were purchasing licenses for the airwaves called spectrum. Naturally, these companies had the deep pockets and the financial resources to bid on and acquire spectrum, build out the markets where the spectrum existed; and continue to grow their businesses. They all wanted spectrum in the major metropolitan areas where more wireless usage-potential existed. That left the smaller markets, which were more costly to serve with less potential, to smaller wireless companies. The FCC saw that as the industry grew, fewer companies would be able to compete with these giants! So, the FCC decided to try to level the playing field in the auction for spectrum. They opened the bidding on a lottery basis to any company that met their criteria.

Larry suggested that Eddie, Larry, and a couple friends (a CPA and an attorney), participate in these cellular auctions. In order to qualify for the FCC auction, you had to have $1 million line letter of credit from the bank, all the insurance necessary to cover the bid if you won it, and have a geological mapping of all the sites identified where the cellular towers would be located. Each member of the group had one of the components necessary to bid in the auction. Eddie's part was the letter of credit.

The government called those that met the qualifications as "throwing your hat in the ring" of a lottery. After that there was a drawing. Every carrier like AT&T had the same amount of voting power as Eddie's little group did. As a result of the lottery Eddie's group actually drew two areas/markets, including the largest city in the state of Mississippi, Jackson, the capital. They also won the rights to a smaller market, which they sold immediately to another carrier. The Jackson market, however, was where they put all of their resources. There were about 10 groups in the same market via this lottery. So if a group would withdraw from the lottery, the next group would take that particular market. Anyone could protest someone else's market to ensure that they really did have the financial, engineering, and insurance resources ready to execute on that particular market.

The next company in the Jackson market protested Eddie's group award indicating that Eddie's group had no contracts on the proposed cellular tower sites. They chose to fight the protest and negotiated a settlement whereby their group combined assets with the protesting group. The strategy all along was to sell their winning market to one of the larger carriers. That did not change!

They ended up selling the market for $800,000 to one of the larger carriers and divided the proceeds between the two groups each receiving $400,000. That meant each individual in Eddie's group received $100,000. Since there was no fee to enter the lottery, every one made $100,000 in a very brief period of time. Eddie has said many times it was the easiest $100,000 he ever made in his life!

In 1993, a young man approached Eddie about starting a car window tinting business as well as installing stereo equipment in the vehicles. Eddie decided to go into the business with a 50/50 partnership.

The business was very successful. He bought a building for the business, put in the equipment and signage, and opened the doors. There was high demand for tinted windshields and sophisticated stereo equipment for cars at that time. The business was called Cool Tint and Auto Décor. His partner did the physical work in the back while Eddie ran the front-end operation, including acquiring new customers. In 1996, Eddie sold his part of the business to his partner. Eddie was able to recoup his investment, make a nice profit, and earned a good salary while he was in the partnership.

Eddie decided to "retire" and use his time and money to build the dream home that he promised his wife, Patsy.

Yet, Eddie always had his hands into the mechanics of vehicles and for years tinkered with cars. In fact, years ago, Eddie had had an opportunity to go to an insurance company car auction with a friend who needed his financial support to buy a car and fix it up. While he was there, Eddie bought a car and refurbished it for himself. This was a hobby that continued throughout Eddie's business career whether he would sell them or just give them away.

EXCEPTIONAL DIMENSION #11
Passion

The key is to follow your heart, but check it with your head!

See page 121 to learn more.

In "retirement", Eddie is still tinkering with cars and has turned his passion for refurbishing cars into a moneymaking business, refurbishing approximately 2 cars per month. This hobby is his final business, which he still actively participates in today.

Eddie persevered through the highs and the lows learning from every experience in his journey, even those that were not successful. Upon refection, Eddie realizes he had too many balls in the air, too many businesses going at the same time between the convenience stores, the trucking company, and the boning plant, plus his "side activities". It's difficult to maintain focus on one business at a time, let alone 3 businesses simultaneously. Visionaries build a plan and remain focused on that plan. Every action taken is to advance that vision, mission, and purpose.

> **EXCEPTIONAL DIMENSION #2**
> **Visionary**
>
> *The key is to create a picture of what success looks like and then build a plan to achieve it!*
>
> See page 80 to learn more.

To summarize, Eddie truly is an *Exceptional Entrepreneur* and great leader who throughout his career was always positive, courageous, hardworking, and passionate. And he still is! *Failure* was never a thought that entered into Eddie's mind. He just did what he needed to do and made things happen.

Because of his innovative and creative approach to business and his great communication, delegation, and decision-making skills, combined with his ability to build productive relationships, he was able to transform his vision into opportunities for success. And most importantly, Eddie's family and his faith supported and guided him in his efforts. It is this to which Eddie gives thanks for his success.

An Interview with Patsy Crouch

No story of an *Exceptional Entrepreneur* is ever complete without gaining insight via another's perspective of success. Also is the case with Eddie Crouch's story. What follows is an interview with Eddie's wife of 50 years, Patsy Crouch. You've read, especially in the early years, how involved Patsy was in the Crouch Meat Company. I felt we could all learn from her perspective what it is like to live and work with an *Exceptional Entrepreneur*.

Author: Can you give me an idea of what it's like to have been married to an *Exceptional Entrepreneur*?

Patsy: Everyday is a challenge. I only dated Eddie for six months before we married and at that time Eddie worked for the Sambol Meatpacking Company. I really didn't know how he was going to turn out. You don't go into a marriage with this type of person thinking you're going to change him. You accept him for the way he is. You don't start out thinking that you're going to change his character. This is the way he was!

Author: If you had known that Eddie was an entrepreneur and working his own business or at least starting his own business, would that have made a difference?

Patsy: No, because I fell in love with the person! Keep in mind I was very young, only 18, when I started dating Eddie and when I married him when I was 19. So no, it would not have made any difference!

Author: So you found out after you were married that this is the way he was?

Patsy: Yes, but I also knew something about him, namely, that he would never be satisfied working for someone else. Never! He always wanted to be out on his own, having his own business. Yes, every day was a challenge because I was the type of person who worried about everything, like where the next paycheck was coming from. I was the person who wanted to save money, while Eddie wants to spend it. He didn't believe in saving money.

Author: Did that create conflict?

Patsy: Not really! Eddie would always look at me and say don't worry about it! It'll be fine!

Author: And you believed him?

Patsy: Yes, because that's just the way he was. To this day, he does not worry about anything.

Author: I know you were an integral part of all of Eddie's businesses. At Crouch Meat, you were the treasurer and paid the bills, you took care of the house payments, you had children to take care of, that's certainly not what you signed up for, was it?

Patsy: Well, overall we got along pretty well! We worked side-by-side. He ran the back of the business and I ran the front. I took care of the sales, the bookkeeping, paying the bills, so naturally I was concerned each day that we'd have enough money to pay the bills. But you know we always seem to make it.

Author: If you had a chance to give advice to a partner of someone who's starting a business, is there anything, besides not trying to change him, you would say to that partner to get the person ready for that experience?

Patsy: One of the things that must be part of that relationship is *trust*. And you have to have a lot of *faith*. I believe that a family that prays together stays together. I feel the same about a business. We would always pray together and each night I would go to bed praying that we would make it through the next day!

As I told you before, every day was a new challenge, facing something new. When a challenge emerged like the meat freeze and our key client, Gilbert Robinson, calling me up to say, "Patsy, what are you going to do about this? You're just a little company! Are you going to be able to supply us?", I was saying to myself, no! And sitting across from me is Eddie saying, yes, we can do this! So, I ended up saying, yes, we can supply you! No problem! Robinson said, "I'll give you until Friday to work this out and if you don't I'll change suppliers."

Eddie got on the phone right away and that day we had worked it out. This was a big deal! But to Eddie it wasn't! He always seems to work it out.

Author: To change subjects, how was life in a trailer for five years?

Patsy: Well, there were times when I would get a little bit down. And of course I was working all that time. I was working retail, I worked in the Diet Center, and I entered the Lancôme Institute in Kansas City.

I finally talked Eddie into selling the acreage so we could use the money to buy a real house. Eddie went to the library and bought this book of drawings and blueprints of houses. He kept looking at all these plans and drawings because he had a bigger house in mind. He told me that he found the house, that I would like it, and it would fit all of our furniture from our previous house. I had never even seen the house before! It was his dream just like everything else that he dreamed about! And even though we found a builder who was going to build our house in trade for our property, Eddie came back after meeting with the builder and said" I'm going to build our own house".

Author: So we have these ideas of *trust, faith, hard work*, right?

Patsy: Yes, you must have in your mind that this is not easy. I told my son just the other day that every job has a certain amount of stress whether you're working for someone or you're on your own. No matter where you are, you'll have challenges to meet.

There are benefits to working for yourself, but you're still going to have lots of challenges and stress. Another factor is that Eddie and I got along very well and agreed on basic issues. Let me give you an example.

One of our veteran employees contracted cancer and went through an extended period of time where she could not work because of her condition. I chose to pay her full salary while she was going through the treatment and Eddie never questioned that decision. In fact, he supported it. Lolly, who was an *exceptional* employee, came to us with the knowledge that she had cancer and thought it was in remission. She told me that before we hired her.

So when the cancer returned, I carried her paycheck to her every week. I can't tell you how long that continued, but I remember when she passed (pause), at the funeral, her husband said how important that pay check was to her.

We didn't have a lot of money. But I would do that again because it was the right thing to do. The reward doesn't come right away. It comes later!

I bring up these things only to point out that with all that was going on in running a business, Eddie was always good to his employees. On more than one occasion, he would buy them cars if they needed transportation. Eddie did these things and never said a word about it. Likewise, he never questioned what I did for Lolly.

So, the most important thing when you consider being in this type of relationship where two people work together side-by-side, is you don't contradict the other person. You might in your mind ask yourself why is he doing that? Or he might say to himself why is she doing something? But we trusted each other and had faith in each other.

Author: In the past you have talked about how important it is to have *patience* (which you learned from your mother) and now, we can add *trust* and *faith* to your list.

Patsy: Yes, and another key is you have to be *honest*. Treat everyone like you want to be treated and always tell the truth even if it hurts.

Author: Patsy, I'm told that you were a great salesperson. Your resume in sales is amazing. You sold real estate, you worked at the Diet Center, you became the sales manager for a real estate company, you started at the Lancôme Institute as part of your cosmetic retail sales career, plus you began your own business selling hairpieces, which had four locations. Least we forget you sold meat for Crouch Meat Company and represented the company at tradeshows. So tell me about your approach to sales that was so successful.

Patsy: My philosophy on selling is simple. It's about making a difference in a person's life, no matter whom you are selling to. It's about touching their life and gaining their faith and trust. If you do that, the sales will come!

Author: I'd say that you are *exceptional* in your own right, Patsy.

Patsy: Thanks, Ed. I'm happy to share my perspective. I appreciate you taking the time with me today.

I believe the verse on the next page represents how Patsy and Eddie Crouch continue to live their lives.
Truly Exceptional!

Living Life

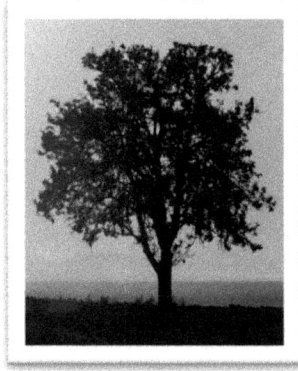

"Life is not a race - but indeed a journey. Be Honest. Work Hard.
Be Choosy. Say 'thank you', and 'great job' to someone each day.
Go to church, take time for prayer. The Lord giveth and the Lord taketh.
Let your handshake mean more than pen and paper.
Love your life and what you've been given, it is not accidental
~ search for your purpose and do it as best you can.
Dreaming does matter. It allows you to become that which you inspire to
be. Laugh often. Appreciate the little things in life and enjoy them.
Some of the best things really are free.
Do not worry, less wrinkles are more becoming. Forgive, it frees the soul.
Take time for yourself ~ Plan for longevity. Recognize the special people
you've been blessed to know. Live for today, enjoy the moment."

www.bonniemohr.com 1-800-264-6647

Family Influence

"He didn't tell me how to live; he lived, and let me watch him do it."
~ Clarence Budington Kelland

As you have read, family was and is an integral and powerful motivator for Eddie Crouch. Throughout his career he did what he did to support and provide for his family. That combined with an entrepreneurial spirit and *exceptional dimensions* led to his vision of success.

A leader, whether that be in business or in a family environment is influential in so many ways. The lesson here is that you should never underestimate the impact you have on others. When I asked Eddie's children about how Eddie has influenced their lives personally and in business, this is what I learned.

It's clear that Eddie's children are very proud of their dad and what he has accomplished. He was always fair and played no favorites. He is a likable person! He would always give a person another chance and never raised his voice in anger.

Although he was very busy with business, he always had time to be a dad and to help others. They say he is a kindhearted and generous man, almost to a fault. There is nothing he wouldn't do for his children, his employees, and others in need. He bought a bus for a school and he even paid private school tuition for an employee's child. At times, his children felt that others may have taken advantage of his generosity. He never saw the bad side of people, only the good. Taking care of his employees and friends earned him respect. This is "his way" and "giving" was an important component to his vision of success. Eddie's children learned how important it is to treat others with kindness, show gratitude, and to see the best in others.

The children recognize that Eddie had great leadership skills and a commanding presence. He could just walk into a room and gain everyone's attention. One of his children said "When I went out on my own, I took from him his leadership, work ethic, and how to run a business."

He was always positive even after he closed his business and had moved into the trailer. He got up in the morning with a smile on his face. He never talked about being down or depressed, never dwelled on the negative. If you asked him, "What now?" He'd just say, "We'll go get it back!" Always optimistic and always *exceptional*!

"I was 12 years old when I first met Eddie Crouch. He hired me to cut his grass. Over time, he let me tag along with him and I learned how to make things happen! He was like a father-figure to me."

~ Pete St. Peter,
Founder/President of PCDI Homes www.pcdi-ks.com

Competency Development

Professional development is very personal. The specific activities that an individual needs to and or wants to impose upon him or herself vary based on their values, needs, desires, and vision of success. Any time there is a gap between your individual goals or objectives versus where you are today in relationship to those objectives, that gap represents a development opportunity.

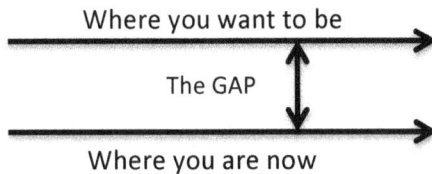

Where you want to be

The GAP

Where you are now

One of the key elements of any development program whether it is about developing leadership skills or competencies to become an entrepreneur, is that it is important to have a good grasp of your own particular strengths and weaknesses.

Many successful leaders have a good idea of areas where they'd like to improve. Entrepreneurs, like Eddie Crouch, also recognize their limitations and areas where they want to concentrate their efforts. But often, as one begins a journey to a successful business career, that may not be the case. Hence, there are tools available that will assist an individual in identifying those strengths and weaknesses.

You can solicit support from trusted people around you to help you measure your effectiveness. For example, a senior member of your team, someone you trust and someone who knows you very well might be an important resource to give you feedback on how you're doing.

Another resource might be a professional coach or someone who could give you feedback after observing you in action. Lastly, you might do a self-assessment or a 360° Feedback Review now and in six months to see if you have moved the needle in a positive way. The "Know Thyself" section starting on page 69 provides more information on assessments and the 360° process.

Once you decide what areas you want to focus on for your development, it's important to document your development plan. Keep it simple. Just create 3 columns. In the first column list the behaviors you want to focus on. In the second column list the developmental actions you need to address, and in the last column add a date in which you will have this action completed. See page 68 for an example of a development plan to get you started. Visit our website at www.mlodzikandcrouch.com to download a blank plan for your own use.

There are a few principles to keep in mind. Limit your areas for development to one or two at a time. Don't try to solve "world hunger"! Take your time and document the activities and the time frames you expect to achieve positive results and once you've mastered those competencies through your development, go on and add others if you need to.

What you've read in this book about Eddie Crouch's entrepreneurship provides a base of information about the behaviors, the characteristics, and the traits, which are necessary to succeed as an entrepreneur and leader. It is up to you to assess where you are in relationship to that potential objective of becoming an entrepreneur and/or a leader whether that be in your own business or in an organization.

What follows are ideas, tools, techniques, and activities to help you create a developmental plan that serves your needs and helps fill the gap between "where you are now" and "where you want to be". You may have to modify them to fit your own personal development. Approach these with the idea that if you can close that gap, you're well on your way to taking that step toward successful entrepreneurship and/or leadership.

EXAMPLE

DEVELOPMENT ACTION PLAN FOR _____ Date: _____

BEHAVIOR FOCUS	DEVELOPMENTAL ACTIONS	TIMELINE (by)
Building Relationships	Probe deeper into issues/concerns using "Question-Listen-Question" techniques. Insure facts are gathered; seek solutions that involve others input. Expect Lead Team to bring solution options when surfacing problems. Seek data to support conclusions / opinions.	Start in current situations and continue with new position by 2nd qtr.
Communications	Build a high-performing team. High integrity, i.e., make a promise; keep it, especially on the "small" things Focus on consistent message and application of principles/values. Read, discuss and apply Lencioni's "5 Dysfunctions of a Team" to reinforce the processes for building trust.	Start with new position and assess in August

Know Thyself!

This section will give an overview of several types of assessments that focus on leadership style and personality. Each will help an individual to know him or herself better. I have used these in my Leadership Coaching and recommend them as a tool to help you understand your strengths and opportunities for development.

Let's define assessment. Assessment is the evaluation or estimation of the nature, quality or ability of someone or something. We are interested in looking at someone's abilities that can impact their success, both positive and negative. Let's start with Blake and Mouton's leadership style assessment which can be found on our website at www.mlodzikandcrouch.com.

Answering a few types of questions can reveal a great deal about your personal leadership style. Some people are very task oriented. They simply want to get things done. Others are very people oriented, and they want people to be happy. Others are a combination of the two. Often it depends on the environment you're in. For example, if you're in an area where enforcing and maintaining tight schedules is paramount, then you'll tend to be more production oriented or task oriented, and you'll need to be that way. In other situations, such as working in a Customer Service department, you may need to make people your priority and accommodate their needs so you'll need to be more people oriented.

Neither preference is right or wrong just as there is no one specific type of leadership style that fits all situations. But understanding what your natural tendencies are can help you develop skills that may be missing in certain environments where you could be more effective. As you will see when you take the assessment, your scores will be placed on a managerial grid with two behavioral dimensions, one where there's a concern for people and another where there's a concern for production. This managerial grid was developed in the 1960s and has stood the test of time as a revealing assessment to prepare an individual for key leadership positions.

There are some specific steps that you can go through to help you identify areas for development. Remember you want to identify your leadership style. At the same time be aware of the situation or environment that you're in or going to that may necessitate modifying or changing your style.

First, think of some recent situations where you were in a leadership position. Second, complete the assessment. Third, since you now know your leadership style, think about whether it suits the situation that you're in. Next, identify ways to reach the leadership position that's warranted in your current environment. Or in the case of an entrepreneur, what areas do you need to improve to be able to exhibit the behaviors that contribute to successful entrepreneurship.

Once you've identified these areas, which in essence is your development plan, work on that particular skill and then monitor your performance and make sure you don't slip back into your preferred style that may be a mismatch. For example, if you tend to be too much on the people orientation, and your position requires much more emphasis on project delivery, you'll have to improve your scheduling process and your work review process in order to achieve results. If you are too task oriented and you see your position will need better communications skills in order to meet the needs of that particular position, then you will have to switch to more of a concern for people and improve your methodology for communicating. See *Exceptional Dimension #3* (Page 85) for ideas to develop your communications skills.

While Blake and Mouton's managerial grid is a practical and useful framework that helps you think about your leadership style, it is not the only answer to the complex challenges of leadership. But it's an excellent starting point and gets one thinking about improving their leadership skills. You can find more information at the following website: http://www.makeadentleadership.com/blake-and-mouton.html

Let's look at a few personality inventories or assessments. You can visit each of their websites to review the one that may be most effective for you. The premise here is once you determine how you are naturally "wired", then you can start to understand how that set of behaviors or personality affects your leadership approach and how you interact with people. Based on findings you may adjust or modify to gain better results.

Kathryn Briggs and her daughter Isabel Briggs Myers, after studying Carl Jung, turned their interest in human behavior into a practical use in the 1940s and although it's been modified over time, the Myers-Briggs assessment helps an individual understand their preferences as it relates to their interest, needs, values, and motivation. The MBTI (Myers-Briggs Type Indicator) sorts through 16 possible psychological types that are outlined on the Myers-Briggs website (www.myersbriggs.org) Basically, these types address Extraversion versus Introversion (E or I), Sensing versus Intuition (S or N), Thinking versus Feeling (T or F), and Judging versus Perceiving (J or P). All of these are put into discernible combinations to help you understand your personality preferences in different situations. If you tie those situations to leadership and entrepreneurship you get a very good idea of how you are wired and how it affects your behavior in given situations. You can then decide how to use what you learned about your personality type to be a more effective leader.

Another assessment that you can review is the DISC. The letters stand for Dominance, Influence, Steadiness, and Conscientiousness. More than 50 million people, a substantial database, but one that is highly diverse, have used the DISC since 1972. It provides insight into one's sense of self and the interaction one has with the environment that he or she finds him or herself in. It helps explain behaviors that could enhance success, or could contribute to failure. Visit www.thediscpersonalitytest.com if you would like to take the DISC test online and receive a report of your personality type. The site will also help you interpret the data so you know the meaning behind the various categories. You can then apply the learnings to your entrepreneurial or leadership environment.

One more personality inventory is the Hogan series. Visit www.hoganassessments.com to gain further information about how to order, complete, and interpret the Hogan assessments. Drs. Robert and Joyce Hogan developed these assessments to focus on executive development. Therefore, your responses to the assessment surveys are linked directly to responses of successful executives. You gain insight into how your leadership, around the various personality scales, relates to the percentage of successful executives who exhibited the same behavior. I have found that the Hogan assessments are best used with someone aspiring to run their own company or a leader working in an executive position or at high organizational level.

I suggest engaging with a Hogan Certified Executive Coach to help you walk through and interpret the results of the surveys. A Leadership Coach that I highly recommend is *Mickie Schroeder: (816) 651-5900, mschroeder721@yahoo.com.* Mickie is certified in these assessments and can give you valuable insight per her experience of debriefing hundreds of people in their assessments. She can also help you put together an effective development plan based on your career objectives and life goals.

Once you gain all this insight about yourself through one or more of these instruments you can begin to see how your personality and behaviors impacts your leadership approach and your relationships with people around you.

Another effective way to gain valuable insights about your strengths and weaknesses is to do a 360° Feedback Survey. It is also known as Multi-Rater feedback or Multi- Source feedback. In addition to several online sources, I recommend that you engage with a Leadership Coach to prepare questions that are directly aligned with the dimensions or competencies that are crucial to achieving your leadership and/or entrepreneurial goals.

The 360° is a very powerful process in which you receive confidential, anonymous feedback covering a range of competencies from the people who work around you (typically your boss, peers, and direct reports – See page 77 for the "In the middle" diagram). The person receiving feedback also fills out a self-rating survey including the same survey questions.

By the way, if you do not have direct reports in your current position, you can send your survey to customers or clients. If you're a student at a university, you can survey your departmental chair, your professors, your fellow students, or people that you work with who know you well. The 360° should be distributed to people that you feel have good insight into your behaviors and actions. If they haven't known you for at least six months or so, they probably don't have the helpful insights.

Your 360° provides you an opportunity to understand how others interpret your actions. Several studies indicate that the use of 360° feedback helps to improve performance because it helps the evaluated see different perspectives of their performance. Things you say or do are constantly being assessed against the other person's frame of reference for better or for worse. In some cases, what you intend is not what is perceived, yet without the use of a 360° instrument, you may not know this is happening. The 360° will help you see where the positive and developmental gaps exist. It is the accumulation of those perceptions and are defined as specific behaviors. It's important to the success of the assessment that those who give feedback remain anonymous and no one including yourself know who said what regarding rating your leadership and competencies. It is also imperative that you distribute to people who know what you're doing and what you are trying to accomplish.

After you have asked for the feedback and "listened" to what the report is telling you, you need to think about it and reflect on understanding how others perceive your behavior and its impact, whether intended or unintended. Be sure to thank participants for taking the time and effort to provide feedback for the report.

Now armed with a personality inventory (how you are wired) and an awareness of how you perform in various competencies that have been evaluated through the 360°, you get a picture of the impact that your behavior is having on the people around you from a leadership perspective. You can then choose to modify the behaviors that can potentially be obstacles and develop the competencies or dimensions that will make you truly *exceptional*.

The 12 Exceptional Dimensions

The following pages outline the 12 *Exceptional Dimensions* that have been highlighted in the story of the *Exceptional Entrepreneur*, Eddie Crouch. These characteristics helped Eddie achieve his vision of success. Within each *Exceptional Dimension*, I have included ideas, activities, and tools that I have used with my clients to develop leadership skills and behaviors.

Not every leader needs to develop all 12 of these competencies. However, it was my experience that 10 out of 12 were common for development! In high-growth companies, technology companies for example, leaders are often given what I call "battle-field promotions". They might have successfully lead a team that designed a new product and as a reward are promoted. A person could end up running a full department! Hence, the leader has a higher wall to climb!

As you read through the definitions of each *Exceptional Dimension*, take time to reflect and assess on how much of this dimension exists in you. Determine if and how you would like to develop each of these characteristics and behaviors based on your situation, career objectives, and life goals. Ask yourself which of these dimensions are most important to your success in your current position or in future endeavors. Then, select no more than two development activities and document them on your **Development Plan**. See page 68 for a sample or visit www.mlodzikandcrouch.com to download and use the tool.

EXCEPTIONAL DIMENSION #1
Building Relationships
The key is to listen first and then deliver on what you heard!

One of the first traits that you encountered in reading the story of Eddie's life was how his father and then later he himself built positive relationships with his clients and business network. For example, Eddie watched his father develop relationships with storeowners when he delivered package meats to their stores. His father knew every person by name, he called on them at the most convenient times, and promoted reliability of service. All of these contributed to solid relationships with his customers.

Eddie learned how important it was to understand the needs of customers, as well as others in his circle of influence, and was always looking for ways to add value and give back. This created trust and loyalty, which was foundational to building positive relationships and creating successful business outcomes.

Eddie developed strong relationships with every Wendy account that he opened and delivered hamburger meat to. He would go to each store and talk with the local manager about the quality of his service. How were we doing? What else can I do to meet your needs? These kinds of questions promoted a dialogue, which enabled Eddie to take positive action to correct any problems. Customer satisfaction was always top priority! You can imagine how this cultivated positive relations with each and every Wendy's location that Crouch Meat served.

How do you assess your degree of competency in this important dimension? First of all, it's a self-assessment. You know yourself and what kind of relationship you have with the people around you. And if you don't, you may want to consider utilizing a 360° assessment (see page 73 for more information).

Like Eddie did, you can ask customers and people around you as series of questions to identify how you are doing. If you are currently working in a company environment, you need to create relationships with those around you. See the "In the middle" diagram below. Above you is your boss, to the right would be your peers (people who work with you or on the same team). To your left would be your customers or clients (internal or external), and below you are your direct reports (the people who work for you). Each point on that compass, and remember you're in the middle, provides an opportunity to build positive relationships.

Your Boss

**Your
Customers**   **You**   **Your
Peers**

**Your Direct
Reports**

So here's the activity. Set time with each group in an office, at lunch, or over coffee, and design questions to help promote the beginnings of a positive relationship. If you're new to your position or if you've not done this with people surrounding you, then you may want to consider the questions on the next page.

Ask your Direct Reports:
- What project/assignment did you most enjoy these past 12 months? Why did you enjoy it so much?
- What skills and talents do you have that you don't think we are fully utilizing?
- What do you expect from me, your direct boss?
- What do you want to know about me?

Ask your Peers:
- What are your job responsibilities?
- What can I do to support you and your team?
- How effective was my Team last year in supporting you?

Ask your Customers/Clients:
- What are your expectations of my team and me?
- What else can we do to deliver exceptional service?
- How did I perform for you last year? Where can we improve?

Ask your Boss:
- What are the top three "must-complete" projects/tasks for this next quarter? Next year?
- What role do you see me fulfilling on your team?
- How often and in what format should we communicate one-on-one?

The fact that you took the time with each of the groups says a great deal about your desire to start building positive relationships. The hard part is first, listening, and the second is delivering on what you heard. Do these two activities well, and people will see your leadership carried out in this *Dimension*.

This will take some time and the more frequently you meet with your peers, your customers, and the people that work for you, the easier this becomes and the better you become at building these relationships. My experience has been that you will begin recognizing the positive power of these meetings and will want to schedule them on a regular, periodic basis to gain best results.

For those of you who are completing school and haven't begun your career in the world of work, you can still use the same relationship building approach. For example, you don't have a boss per se. Yet, you do have the Dean of your particular college curriculum, you may not have direct reports, but you do have members of a study team or project team that you can work with on relationship building. Your peers could be anyone from a roommate to a social organization or group that you belong to. It's never too early to start building relationships.

As you recall, Eddie was able to secure a loan for a small panel truck. He could only do that because he had established a good positive working relationship with the local bank. And throughout his career, Eddie was able to secure a letter of credit for beginning a number of his enterprises. Again, a bank is only going to meet those requests for people they have a positive working relationship with. As someone starting a career and contemplating creating your own business, begin to assess and build relationships with those around you, in school, in your community and continue to nurture those relationships while developing new ones throughout your business career.

The more you practice using the "in the middle" questions to those people around you, the more you will be able to comfortably prepare yourself for business relationships. You may have to modify these questions depending upon the group or the individuals in your circle of influence or to the situation. However, the bottom line is that you want to generate a network of positive relationships that endures over time and helps you to deliver successful results.

EXCEPTIONAL DIMENSION #2
Visionary
*The key is to create a picture of what success looks like and
then build a plan to achieve it!*

Entrepreneurs are dreamers! They see in their minds what they want to accomplish or they create the dream when the see it! A Visionary creates a compelling picture of the future. They articulate that picture to employees, bankers, customers, or whoever has the greatest need to understand the direction.

When Eddie saw the opportunity to purchase his first meat processing facility, he could see the space with equipment and employees producing his products. When Eddie decided to specialize in hamburger (ground beef), he had already visualized what the benefits were in choosing that product line.

In order to communicate his vision, the leader needs to create a Mission or Purpose statement. Then he needs to create a plan to make it happen!

The next time you watch the winter sport of downhill skiing, watch the skier at the top of the run, before she/he starts. The skier is moving through the course, visualizing the run and taking every turn before the start. The vision is victory!

Let's define Visionary:

- Thinking about or planning the future with imagination or wisdom.

- Having or showing clear ideas about what should happen or be done in the future.

A Visionary person will create a mission statement for his/her organization and a Personal Mission statement for their own life. This is a thoughtful process that takes time and deliberation, but once written, enables the Visionary person to function based of principles.

The Business Visionary creates a Mission or Purpose statement to communicate their vision.

In their simplest form, mission statements articulate the purpose of an organization. Many organizations use the terms "mission" and "purpose" interchangeably. Mission statements should capture the essence of excellence. They should inspire. When others read your mission statement, they will know what success "looks like" for your company or department.

What a Vision / Mission Statement contains:

- Emphasis on what you do, not how you do it

- High standards and expectations for performance

- Unique characteristics – what the team wants to be known for

- Future orientation

- The creation of a "mind's eye" image

- The provision of a sense of unity

To draft your mission statement, complete these sentences:

- I believe our company's or team's purpose is to _____.

- Our team supports the company's mission by_____.

To test your draft, consider the following criteria:

- Does it describe *what* the team does, not how the team does it?

- Does it inspire your team to excellence?

- Can you "see" what success looks like for your team?

- Is it aligned – both horizontally (with other departments) and vertically (with the Organization) – with other mission statements?

- Does it point to the future?

- Does it unify Team Members and their activities?

<u>The Individual Visionary</u> creates a Personal Mission Statement

A Personal Mission statement is like a constitution by which you make decisions for how you live *your* life. In other words, you shape your future by following your Mission Statement. Steps to create your Personal Mission Statement:

1. Identify and list the roles you fulfill in your life. For example, the role of parent, neighbor, community volunteer, church member, etc.

2. Next, write what a key person in each role would say about you as a tribute to your performance in that role.

3. Think about what you do when you are at your best? When you are at your worst? Document your natural talents. Write down what you really love to do in your personal life.

4. Think about the people in your life and how they influenced you.

Now, put all these thoughts and lists in front of you and begin to write a draft of your Personal Mission Statement. Once your draft is completed, revise and refine it. To help with this final step, you may want to read biographies of people who have accomplished what you'd like to achieve.

This process is contained in Habit 2 of Stephen Covey's *7 Habits of Highly Effective People.*

The following are some additional thoughts from *7 Qualities of Visionary Leadership* by Brian Tracy:

1. **Leaders inspire others because they are inspired themselves.** They are excited about the possibility of creating an exciting future for themselves. Leaders get up every morning and they see every effort they make as part of a great plan to accomplish something wonderful with their lives.

2. **Leaders are optimistic.** They see opportunities in everything that happens, positive or negative. Leaders look for the good in every situation and in every person. They seek the valuable lessons contained in every problem or setback. They never experience "failures" instead, they write them off as "learning experiences" and move on with positivity and enthusiasm.

3. **Leaders have a sense of meaning and purpose in each area of their lives.** They have clear goals and plans they work on every day. Leaders are clear about where they are going and what they will have to do to get there. Their behavior is purposeful and goal-directed. As a result, they accomplish five and ten times as much as the average person who operates from day to day with little concern about the future.

4. **Leaders accept personal responsibility.** Leaders never complain, never explain. Instead of making excuses, they make progress. Whenever they have a setback or difficulty, they repeat to themselves, "I am responsible! I am responsible! I am responsible!"

5. **Leaders see themselves as victors over circumstances rather than victims of circumstances.** They don't criticize or blame others when something goes wrong. Instead, they focus on the solution.

6. **Leaders are action-oriented.** They are constantly in motion. They try something, and then something else, and then something else again. They never give up.

7. **Leaders have integrity.** They tell the truth at all times. They live in truth with themselves, and they live in truth with others.

As I read through the 7 qualities above, it's clear that Eddie was an *Exceptional Visionary!*

EXCEPTIONAL DIMENSION #3
Communication
The key is consistency, impact, and clarity: consider what, who, when, where, and how your communications will be delivered most effectively!

Communications is a skill and a set of behaviors that are critical in establishing and maintaining a business. Plus, these are key leadership components for anyone in a position within an organization where people are involved. And that's just about any position!

Part of communications is ensuring that what ever message you are trying to communicate to your organization, to your company's employees, to the general public, are carefully thought out and consistent. For example, when Eddie purchased the facility in St. Joseph, Missouri for his meatpacking plant, the local press was waiting to interview Eddie because of the impact that this business would have on the local community. There were numerous employment positions at stake! Eddie's communication style and message during those early moments of his purchase were optimistic and reassuring without making any specific commitments or statements that would mislead the general public.

The 5-question formula for planning communications:

1. **What is it you want to say?** Is it to announce a new product, a new direction for your business, and expansion,

whatever the content is for your message needs to be documented.

2. **Whom do you intend to communicate with and in what kind of forum?** General public, employees, the newspaper press, who will be the recipient of the content?

3. **When do you intend to communicate your message?** At a dinner, the morning meeting, in your staff meeting, etc. Give some thought to the potential duplication and necessity of doing this communicating more than once, in different settings.

4. **How will you communicate your message?** What media do you intend to use? How do the people listening to your message prefer to receive your communications? This might include a number of different methods. For example, you might want to publish your message on your website for general public distribution. Or you might want to use a broadcast voicemail so that everyone in your organization receives notice that they have a message when they arrive the next morning. Or you might want to distribute a carefully crafted email that could go out to a number of different groups of people or individuals.

In other words, carefully consider what, who, when, where, and how your communications will be delivered most effectively. The **Communications Planning Template** on page 87 is a great tool to use as part of your communications planning. Visit our website at www.mlodzikandcrouch.com to download and keep in your communications toolbox. Consistency, impact, and clarity are all critical to any business success on an ongoing basis when you're getting your message out.

EXAMPLE

Communication Planning Template			
When to use: Any time you have a significant message to deliver that you need people to absorb, you'll want to use this planning document. Due to the volume of disjointed data that people are exposed to via e-mail, wireless technology, cubicle noise, deadlines and multi-tasking, it has become infinitely harder to deliver a consistent message and expect retention. Statistics tell us that, in order to assume retention and expect people to take action or change behavior, you will need to deliver the message at least seven times – preferably in different mediums. This tool will help you identify the urgency of your message and create a simple communication plan to improve the chances that people "get it".			
How to use: Review the questions and provide the answers in the below columns considering your target audience to help you plan your communications.			
Who is your audience?	**What** do you need to communicate?	**When** will you communicate and follow up?	**How** will it be delivered?
My Team	Convey key quarterly results through the Manager Talking Points in the newsletter, reinforce in email messaging, (what's changing, what's not). Ask for pre-submitted ideas to improve results. (Anonymously submitted or e-mailed to me.) Answer questions in staff meeting.	Monday team meeting. Follow up via e-mail in afternoon with highlights and Q&As.	Team meeting Follow up w/e-mail and phone calls

Communications are also critical in building relationships and most critically, in one-on-one conversations with a person who has the most influence or impact on you. For those of you who are currently in an organization, that person would probably be your immediate supervisor or boss. If you're in graduate school, it might be your advisor or the Dean of your particular department. If you are running your own business, it might be your Board of Directors or specifically a member of that board that you're basically reporting to. Regardless, these situations warrant a more targeted and focused communication.

In these situations, I'd like you to consider using the **Contract for Success** seen on page 91 that is a useful tool for planning your communications. You can also download it from our website at www.mlodzikandcrouch.com.

What makes this particular communications tool even more effective is to give a blank contract to the individual you intend to communicate with. Ask the person to complete their perception of your top tasks or objectives, what they perceive your role to be, and how they want to communicate with you. Then when you sit down one-on-one take the contracts out and compare yours and theirs. It affords an excellent opportunity to communicate and clarify any differences.

This tool is designed to be open one-on-one communications. It's especially effective if you were newly appointed to your current position. However, I have seen it effectively used with seasoned managers and their direct reports.

The Contract is divided into three sections:

1. **Objectives** – First, document the two or three most critical deliverables or objectives that you are trying to accomplish in your position. These would include overall company

objectives right down to individual specific objectives that you want to ensure the person that you report to agrees with. Don't forget to include when those deliverables or objectives will be completed.

2. **Role** – The next component gives you an opportunity to document and therefore communicate what you see your role to be in this current position. That role might be to become the leader in the industry all the way to being a change agent in your company. But give some thought to what you feel your role is.

3. **Preference on communication** – The last component documents how you want this person to communicate to you, namely, how frequently, for how long a period of time, and in what environment. Will it be weekly meetings with this individual, will it be a monthly phone call to review results, what is the best way for you to communicate with this individual?

One final thought regarding communications: do not forget that part of communications is *listening*. In one-on-one conversations, the concentration needed and acknowledgment that you have heard what the other person is trying to convey in any conversation is just as important as the concentration and focus one injects into their message and how it's delivered. The principle around good listening is to ensure that you totally understand what you heard before you convey your message. Make every effort to playback the words, the meaning of the words, and the specific meaning of what the individual has just said to you. Once the other party has had knowledge that yes, you've heard me, then you can respond.

This communication skill requires practice. Our education regarding communication is strongest in the written format, programs and courses about verbal communications, and weakest in providing listening techniques. This means that most people do not have a formal listening course or study available to them. But let me suggest that one of the best listening programs is from the famous *Seven Habits of Highly Effective People* by Dr. Stephen Covey. Habit number five, *Seek First to Understand, Then to be Understood*, contains numerous examples and practices to enhance your listening skills.

So read it! Study it! Work on it! Did you hear me!?!

Effective communication also includes the way we present our material and ourselves. Let's recognize that we can all improve our presentation skills. How comfortable we are in front of groups, what visuals we use to present our ideas, how attentive we are to our audience, all these skills are important and go beyond basic communications. There are numerous Presentation Skills seminars usually offered at local universities or consulting firms throughout the calendar year. In addition, I recommend that you consider a Presentations/Communications Coach, a person who can work with you one-on-one on techniques, rehearse with you and give you feedback on your presentations. Most of these professionals have their own websites and therefore you can search them out on the internet. In addition, the International Coaching Federation should have a local chapter in your location that can provide valuable resources.

The Contract for Success

Expectations	Measure of Success	Due Date
What are your top 3 objectives? From your point of view, list the results expected of you this year. "I am expected to…."	Identify how you believe your boss will be measuring your performance.	What do you believe is the timetable for achieving these results?

Your Unique Role

Define how you think your unique role adds value to the mission / purpose for this team. Would your boss agree? Consider how you will interact with various groups (peers, team, boss, other departmental teams, etc.), vendors, organizational culture and change, relationship with boss, scope of influence, politics, decision-making, etc.

Communicating With Your Boss

List how you will communicate the above objectives and updates to your boss. Voice mail, e-mail, weekly 1:1's? When will you escalate and when does your boss want to be left alone?

Employee:_____ Date:_____

Manager:_____ Date:_____

EXCEPTIONAL DIMENSION #4
Decision-making
The key is to make your decision sound and do it rapidly!

Another critical dimension of a successful entrepreneur is the ability to make sound business decisions rapidly. There are two components: *sound decision-making* and *doing it rapidly.*

During his career, Eddie had to make numerous decisions under the pressure of time in order to meet the opportunity. Hence, he was able to formulate sound businesses by making the best possible decision. For example, Eddie had to make a decision to purchase the meatpacking plant. That decision was made during an auction, with very little time to do a thorough analysis. It was a "go or no go" decision. You weigh the risk versus the potential and making up your mind about a given opportunity. In Eddie's case, in order to expand his business, he needed the space to accommodate additional customers and clients for his product and services. The opportunity presented itself; he carefully weighed the considerations, and decided to go with.

When making a "go or no go" decision, you review the risk versus the reward, review your own personal criteria for that particular opportunity, and you decide to do it or not.

More complex are the decisions needed to select against several alternatives. This requires a process, which you can practice, and apply to many different situations. The process is outlined on the next page:

1. **Develop a statement of what the decision is going to be.** For example, am I going to buy a sports car, a sedan, or a SUV? My statement isn't elaborate it's just simply knowing where to go with my decision.

2. **Identify the alternatives.** In my example the alternatives are three different types of vehicles. It could be three different suppliers. It could be three different customers. Whatever the number of alternatives, list them so that you know what you're facing in the way of making a decision.

3. **Develop criteria that you will use to make your decision.** Most importantly within that criteria, develop any eliminators. These eliminators are critical! They are the must-have's regardless of what alternative you select. In my example one eliminator might be, "must have four doors". Add other criteria then once the eliminator is satisfied you can move on. For example, now that I know I must get a vehicle with four doors, I can add certain fuel efficiency, type of warranty, ease of driving, visibility, etc. Now when I look at my choices (sports car, a sedan, or a SUV), I've already eliminated the sports car. I can begin to focus in on the four-door sedan or the four-door SUV.

4. **Add numerical value to your criteria.** Once you review your criteria then identify the one that is more important (10) and the one that is least important (1). In other words, put some type of value on all the criteria and actually, apply a numerical value to each criterion. For example, it might be worth a 10 to me for superior fuel economy. It might only be worth a 5 to me as far as visibility is concerned. And so on throughout your criteria.

5. **Evaluate each alternative against your criteria and give each alternative score.** For example the SUV might have

only a value of 6 in terms of visibility and 4 in terms of fuel economy, while the sedan might have a 9 score on both. I merely then take that alternative score times the value of the criteria and add up my scores. Whichever alternative has the highest score wins.

This might sound rather cumbersome, and it may seem like it's taking too much time so please see page 95 for the **Decision-Making Matrix** developed by Action Management Associates, Inc. (www.actionm.com). It is a helpful tool that is laid out just like the process that I described. You may also visit our website at www.mlodzikandcrouch.com to download the matrix. The point of the process is to practice it in different situations where a decision is necessary. For example, Eddie decided what his product would be comparing hamburger meat to all the different types of meat. The process of manufacturing hamburger only was weighed against carrying all types of meat products. You can imagine the cost of manufacturing, the ease in packaging, delivery challenges, were some of the criteria that Eddie used when he decided to become the best producer of hamburger.

A suggestion here might be to take a simple decision that you have to make and run it through the process. You might find it interesting in terms of identifying the alternatives and assessing which is the best one to decide upon. For example, I've seen people use this process in planning where to go on vacation. I've heard of folks using this process to buy a home when there are several choices available. Whatever the process is that you're practicing on, you can engage others in that process as well. The more you practice it, the faster you become in applying the process. Therefore, you are increasing the velocity of your decision-making, while at the same time improving the quality of your decisions. And, now you have strong rationale for your decision.

Decision Making Matrix

Clear | Increase Input Area | Process Flow | Print Matrix

Decision Statement:

Eliminators:

Criteria | Alternatives

Wgt. | Sc. | Wgt. | Sc. | Wgt. | Sc. | Wgt. | Sc. | Wgt. | Sc.

Total Score

EXCEPTIONAL DIMENSION #5
Courage
The key is taking chances and proceeding
with them despite the obstacles that lie ahead!

Courage is an attribute that takes on different definitions in different situations. For the entrepreneur, it applies to making risky decisions, staying the course through difficult times, bouncing back after failures, and a host of day-to-day events that test the entrepreneur's mettle.

It is an attribute of good character. Entrepreneurs will take financial risks to follow their dreams and are like modern day knights that exemplify the rewards that courage can bring. There are different types of courage, ranging from physical strength and endurance to mental stamina and innovation.

Standing up for what is right is another positive way to demonstrate courage. For example, as you read in the interview with Eddie's wife, Patsy, she continued to pay an outstanding employee who could not work because of suffering with cancer. She did it because it was the right thing to do. And that took courage, acting on her convictions according to her beliefs.

Robert Frost once said, "Freedom lies in being bold." And being bold sometimes requires a great deal of courage. When Eddie purchased the bankrupt meat packing plant, which became the foundation for the Crouch Meat Company, he made a bold move, a risky decision, and with the confidence of his belief in himself.

Courage today is to take chances and proceed with them despite the obstacles that lie ahead. Following one's dreams without the fear of what will happen tomorrow was essential in many of the decisions that Eddie made throughout his entrepreneurial career. And even if something failed in those efforts, he just tried harder the next day to make those dreams happen.

Courage is the ability to accept change from these risks and succeed without changing who we are. The *Serenity Prayer* says it best. "God grant me the serenity to accept the things I cannot change; courage to change the things I can, and wisdom to know the difference."

There are no classes or seminars on how to acquire courage. But one can look for opportunities to stand by friends, family, or employees during challenging circumstances coaching them, listening to them, and supporting them. In a sense one learns to handle our own confidence and fears figuring out the right thing to do, and mustering the will to do it.

Look for those opportunities where in low risk environments you can practice taking a stand on a current issue, discussing your stance with a person you respect and one who admires you. Get a sense of how it feels to take that position, and win or lose the debate; practice what you need to feel confident in taking your position.

Remember, this is not physical courage. This is standing behind your convictions, being able to realize your dreams, overcome obstacles, bounce back from being sidetracked, and continuing on your entrepreneurial journey.

And William Bennett's *Book of Virtues* there are countless stories and essays that exemplify courage as we define it in a business reality sense. The following is a poem by Alice and Phoebe Cary, *Our Heroes*, that exemplifies seeing what is right and doing it with firm resolve despite the opinions of the crowd.

Here's a hand to the boy who has courage
To do what he knows to be right;
When he falls in the way of temptation,
He has a hard battle to fight.
Who strives against self and his comrades
Will find a most powerful foe;
All honor to him if he conquers—
A cheer for the boy who says "No!"
There's many a battle fought daily
The world knows nothing about;
There's many a brave little soldier
Whose strength puts a legion to rout.
And he who fights sin single-handed
Is more of a hero, I say,
Than he who leads soldiers to battle,
And conquers by arms in the fray.
Be steadfast, my boy, when you're tempted
And do what you know to be right;
Stand firm by the colors of manhood,
And you will overcome in the fight.
"The Right" be your battle-cry ever,
In waging the warfare of life;
And God, who knows who are the heroes,
Will give you the strength for the strife.

Innovation

The key is to be creative and use a synergistic approach to develop new ideas that are impactful and satisfy needs of the market!

In today's business world, a key measure of success relates to sustainability of a business. One of the key components that contribute to sustainability is innovation. In other words, the entrepreneur creates a business and then sustains it through constant innovation going forward.

Let's define our terms. Innovation is the process of translating an idea or invention into a good or service that creates value or for which customers will pay. To be called an innovation, an idea must be replicable at an economical cost and must satisfy a specific need.

When we apply this definition to Eddie's entrepreneurship, there are several specific examples of how innovation helped build and sustain his business. For example, after purchasing the bankrupt meatpacking plant, with its refrigerated interior, Eddie saw the possibilities of utilizing that space to help solve a problem the US government was having related to cheese storage. Another example would be when he made the decision to specialize his product and become the best hamburger producer in the area. These are examples of sustaining his businesses into new markets with new products to meet the needs of a changing marketplace or customer base. It's what brought about the success he had in acquiring the supplier position for the Wendy's franchise.

Creativity is a core competency for entrepreneurs, and a crucial component of the innovation equation. Creativity requires whole-brain thinking; right-brain imagination, artistry and intuition, plus left-brain logic and planning.

So how does one develop creativity that leads to innovation? Fortunately, there are many resources available to help an individual master the techniques and ideas that build creativity. Seminars and classes are available (search on the Internet for innovative/creative seminars, and take your pick!).

If you lead a team or are involved with a group working on a project, value creative ideas! Use a synergistic approach to develop creative ideas. In the book by Stephen Covey, *The Seven Habits of Highly Effective People*, a full chapter is devoted to Habit 6: Synergize. In its basic format, to synergize is taking two ideas and making a third idea. That new idea should be greater in terms of impact then the other ideas taken alone. Covey uses the formula of "1 + 1= 3" to show the concept of "two heads are better than one" and creative cooperation.

Another activity that stimulates innovation and creativity is actually taking time out to do whole brain thinking. If you schedule every hour of every day in some type of work activity, you can lose your creativity so set aside some unstructured time that you can devote to *thinking*.

Read stories about innovative leaders. Peter Drucker has written several books on *Managing for the Future*. Joel Barker has written the book entitled, *Paradigms: the Business of Discovering the Future*. And lastly, *Recapturing the Spirit of Enterprise* by George Gilder is loaded with stories about innovative leaders.

It becomes obvious that innovation and creativity are components tied to being a visionary, building strong relationships, communicating effectively (including listening), and generally developing a mindset where you're constantly looking for new business opportunities or expanding on your success with new products and services. So, ask better questions, collaborate effectively, and enroll others in your ideas.

In conclusion, I can honestly attest to the fact that I don't have a creative bone in my body! But my team at Sprint generated many creative processes and coaching products. They were the creative ones! So my role (and yours, if you're like me!) was to provide a forum that stresses being innovative, to reward new creative and effective ideas, to recognize success, and to keep the fires of innovation burning.

EXCEPTIONAL DIMENSION #7
Hard working
The key is keeping your foot on the gas
so your competitor does not move in!

This dimension is phrased as an adjective. It describes the behavior of successful entrepreneurs. Hard working comes with establishing one's own business and maintaining it over an extended period of time.

Where does one gain the reputation of being hard-working? Often it's tied to an occupation, such as farming. In that occupation, a person works from dawn to dusk, takes lunch in the field, manages the farm at different times, in the evening, during bad weather, or whenever the farmer can work it in. There is no "overtime" in farming; it's all hard work. Hard work in a corporate setting may include arriving at the office several hours before others arrive and/or staying several hours after others leave. The output of that time is reflected in the quality of staff work completed. These are observable situations where an individual becomes known as a "hard worker".

Let's be sure that you understand that starting your own business requires hard work. And as George Gilder says in his book, *Recapturing the Spirit of Entrepreneurship,* you have to keep working hard because "the minute you take your foot off the gas, your competitor moves in." So this attribute of an entrepreneur is more of a commitment to working hard.

How does one learn to work hard? Where does one create a work ethic? Most people learn about hard work by watching their parents or family members strive toward reaching a particular goal or purpose in life. As an adult that can translate into being a model for younger people so that they are able to see what hard work really is.

So let's define hard work. In William J. Bennett's book, *The Book of Virtues*, he says work is effort applied toward something and the most satisfying work involves directing our efforts toward achieving ends that we ourselves endorse as worthy expressions of our talent and character. The dictionary defines hard working as an adjective "…tending to work with energy and commitment: diligent". Some synonyms for hard working include industriousness, untiring, tireless, and conscientious.

If you study an entrepreneur or you work in a small business started by an entrepreneur, you'll notice that hard working also means that everyone in a small organization contributes to the overall vision. And what that means is that everyone including the owner/president does whatever is necessary to keep that business going. It's not uncommon that the president of the organization is dealing directly with an important client in the morning and later in the day is taking out the trash from the warehouse. Or the chief financial officer, the accountant, is also responsible for doing all the mailing or direct mail pieces that go out to the business community. This is my observation as it relates to hard working. It sets a tone for all the employees that simply says, if I need you to shovel the front steps, even though it's not written down, that's your job and you will grab a shovel to clean off the front steps. That's a working hard ethic.

For those of you who need to develop a hard working attitude, I recommend reading the essay by Charles Edison, about his brother Thomas Edison, entitled, *It's plain hard work that does it.*

The essay provides some interesting insights into the work habits of the Edison family.

Also, there's an interesting quote from Ade Bethune that I think summarizes the whole approach to work.

"I went back to being an amateur, in the sense of somebody who loves what she's doing. If a professional loses the love of work, routine sets in, and that's the death of work and of life."

EXCEPTIONAL DIMENSION #8
Resilience
The key is to bounce back quickly from
derailments and major disruptions!

Key to a successful career as an entrepreneur is adopting the necessary behaviors to cope with setbacks, those occasions where things do not work out as planned, opportunities take a different direction, or professional or personal obstacles get in the way of success.

During Eddie's career you have read about his continued success in capturing those opportunities and turning them into successful businesses. But as in most entrepreneurial quests, Eddie suffered setbacks in his career. His convenience store effort was derailed; he lost the Wendy's account, and suffered several personal tragedies along the way. What is noticeable is how after the setbacks, Eddie reacted in a positive way, turning a negative into a positive business development opportunity. So, let's review this characteristic called resiliency and determine where you are in your own resiliency efforts. Then we'll look at different characteristics of a resilient person and identify ways to increase your effectiveness if there is a deficiency.

First a few definitions: resilience is the ability to absorb high levels of disruptive change while displaying minimal dysfunctional behavior. Therefore, when things go wrong in your life and career is disrupted you are allowed to be upset, but not to the point that it disrupts your efforts to recover.

Another definition: resilience is the force that allows people to go beyond survival and to actually prosper in environments that are becoming increasingly complex. Recall in Eddie's life when he acquired the facility for his meatpacking company, he discovered an opportunity to work with the government and help distribute a large quantity of cheese. All of a sudden, he faced obstacles, like railroad tracks sinking, and had to adapt quickly in order to survive.

There are five characteristics of resiliency:

1. **Solutions-Oriented/Positive** – display self-assurance based on a view of life as complex but filled with opportunity. Refer to page 124 for *Exceptional Dimension #12, Positive Attitude* as it contributes to this characteristic.

2. **Visionary/Focused** – have a clear vision of what is to be achieved. Entrepreneurs like Eddie can look at a given situation as a true opportunity and see the potential in that business. Refer to page 80 for *Exceptional Dimension #2, Visionary.*

3. **Adaptable/Flexible** – demonstrate a special pliability and adaptability when responding to uncertainty. There were several occasions in Eddie's career where this characteristic is demonstrated. For example, he had quickly seen several choices or options that his company could take when the government implemented a freeze on meat.

4. **Structured/Organized** – develop structured approaches to managing ambiguity. Eddie never sat down and drew up an organized plan on paper. But what he did do as part of his way of having an approach to managing adversity was to take action, to problem solve, to look for solutions and

not dwell on the past. In a sense this was his method of managing ambiguity and organizing a plan of action.

5. **Proactive** - engaged change rather than defend against it. In other words, instead of reacting, a resilient entrepreneur will seize the opportunity and create action. Change does not derail the entrepreneur permanently. It's just a mild turn on the road to success.

To help you measure your resiliency, see page 109 for the **Personal Resilience Profile Assessment**. This tool was developed by Organizational Development Resources (ODR). You can also download it from our website at www.mlodzikandcrouch.com.

The characteristics of resilient people exist in every one in varying degrees. The real key to being resilient is to have a balance among these characteristics. For example, if a person is extremely flexible but scores low in the area of focus, that person may look at numerous options in responding to change but without being able to make a decision. So the objective is to strive for balance. These characteristics, when you combine them together, enable a person to bounce back quickly from derailments and major disruptions in their lives.

Before you take the Personal Resilience Profile Assessment, answer these two questions:

1. Which of the resilience characteristics do you believe to be your strongest?

2. Which of the characteristics may be out of balance in your work life or student life?

Now, take the assessment. When complete, compare your responses to the 2 questions to your scores on the assessment instrument. Once you review this feedback and compare it to your answers to the questions, take a few moments and list on your development plan possible steps you could take to enhance your resilience.

When reviewing your assessment results, look for balance. If you see one of the characteristics higher than the others and low in the other, then you are putting too much emphasis on the one and not enough on the other. For example, if you score high on Adaptability and low in Visionary, you may have trouble making a clear decision when you have too many options.

If your score is low on Structured compared to the others, then you need to develop more structure into your day-to-day managing activities and not present a "shooting from the hip" image.

All five characteristics of resilient people (Solutions-oriented, Visionary, Adaptable, Structured, and Proactive) when functioning together give an individual the behavior to respond to change and/or adversity without displaying high levels of dysfunctionality.

Laura Hillenbrand is my favorite author who writes about people who overcome great obstacles. Her book, *Unbroken*, is a great read with countless examples of the main character overcoming great obstacles and bouncing back against severe ambiguity. And if you've seen the movie *Seabiscuit*, based on her book of the same name, you learn several ways different characters (real people) overcame obstacles. Plus, they are both entertaining and exciting stories.

Personal Resilience Assessment

Rating Scale	1 = Not at all 2 = To a little extent	3 = To some extent 4 = To a great extent	5 = To a very great extent	
Section I: Solutions-Oriented				Score
1	I feel that he/she is creative when faced with problems.			
2	His/Her solutions to problems presented by change are realistic.			
3	When faced with change, I feel that he/she will eventually be able to find a solution to the problem.			
4	He/She explores several options before settling on a solution to a problem.			
5	His/Her team and he/she engage in creative, problem-solving methods to create a plan.			
6	He/She is focused on solutions.			
		TOTALS SECTION I - SOLUTIONS-ORIENTED		
Section II: Visionary				
7	When dealing with change, he/she is goal-oriented.			
8	He/She is able to see the "big picture."			
9	He/She uses methodical, strategic approaches to change situations.			
		TOTALS SECTION II - VISIONARY		
Section III: Adaptable				
10	During change, he/she adjusts to new circumstances.			
11	When discussing options, he/she is open to different viewpoints.			
12	His/Her skills and abilities are multi-faceted so that he/she can do what's needed as conditions change.			
13	He/She acts flexibly in the face of difficulties.			
		TOTALS SECTION III - ADAPTABLE		
Section IV: Structured				
14	He/She uses Sprint tools, processes, and systems to plan and implement change.			
15	When situations are uncertain and changing, he/she uses problem-solving methods to identify what needs to be done.			
16	He/She anticipates change and methodically plans for it.			
17	Once he/she determines what to do, he/she identifies the tactics he/she will use to accomplish his/her objectives.			
18	He/She executes his/her plans in accordance with his/her goals and objectives.			
		TOTALS SECTION IV - STRUCTURED		
Section V: Proactive				
19	He/She finds that it is extremely important to consistently stay in touch with his/her customers.			
20	He/She spends a significant amount of time observing and interpreting trends so that he/she can be prepared for the need for change.			
21	He/She is more action-oriented than most.			
22	He/She feels that taking reasonable risks should be encouraged and rewarded.			
23	He/She often plans for change rather than reacts to it.			
24	He/She feels that change is inevitable, therefore it is important to actively pursue change in organizations.			
		TOTALS SECTION V - PROACTIVE		

EXCEPTIONAL DIMENSION #9
Delegation
The key is to make the best use of your time and skills and to help other people develop to their full potential!

Delegation is a behavior as well as a skill that contributes to the successful running of a business. Before we officially define it let's talk a little bit about the general uses of delegation.

One of the biggest challenges a client of mine had in making the transition to leading (versus doing) is "letting go!" The leader must resist jumping in and doing it him/herself! It's time to check the ego at the door and not demonstrate how good you are at a particular task! It's time to delegate!

First, delegation can be an effective training tool for a leader to begin the process of training his successor. Second, delegation can also increase the number of "Go-To" people in a particular leaders employee group. Let me explain.

Most leaders have one or two people in their organization that because of their experience and their proven skills makes them a natural to delegate important tasks. These people have the advantage of their experience when it comes to being assigned important tasks. The danger for the leader is that they always get the most meaningful assignments and the leader, in doing so, fails to develop more depth, more "Go-To" people in his organization. Yes, it's the safe way and allows the manager or the leader more time to devote to other tasks. There's no question that assigning the more meaningful, difficult tasks to the less experienced people will require closer coaching and training on the part of the manager. This takes time. But the time invested now will expand the number of people that a manager can count on when the chips are down and tasks need to be delegated.

Sometimes, you have no choice! When Eddie began his meat company, his only employees were his son and his wife, Patsy. So he assigned Patsy the job of sales. Now Patsy had plenty of sales experience but she knew nothing about selling meat. So Eddie had to devote time to train Patsy on his product and then she was ready to sell the product. His delegation process was a training opportunity as well as delegating the responsibility of sales.

So you can see that the behavior/skill of delegation will vary depending on the situation. Let's define our terms:

Delegation is the assignment of responsibility or authority to another person (normally from a manager to a subordinate) to carry out specific activities. However, the person who delegated the work remains accountable for the outcome of the delegated work.

Delegation empowers a subordinate to make decisions, i.e. it is a shift of decision-making authority from one organizational level to a lower one. Delegation, if properly done, is not abdication. The opposite of effective delegation is micromanagement, where a manager provides too much input, direction, and review of delegated work. So the objective is to provide good, positive delegation.

Good delegation saves money, time, builds people and team skills, grooms successors and motivates people. Poor delegation sucks! Ask any employee. It causes frustration, demotivates and confuses people and teams. It is important to develop good delegation skills.

To assist you in the important task of delegation, see page 116 for the **Delegation Discussion Guide**. Be sure to visit www.mlodzikandcrouch.com to download. This tool is a guide. It does not have to be actually filled out; it can be used like a checklist to ensure all the important points of good positive delegation are covered. However, depending on the situation, you might want to complete it and after the delegation discussion is over or give it to the person you've delegated the task to. Either way, it's important to cover all the essential points, as delegation can be a challenge in communications. And remember some people you are delegating to will require more coaching or training then more experienced people. So be flexible and apply the discussion guide to your situation.

Let's review the guide, which is divided into three major sections. On the right-hand side, space has been provided to use during your reviews.

The first section, Context, sets the context of the delegation assignment. It includes purpose, any necessary background that the person needs to be aware of (urgency, politics, etc.). And don't forget to include why you're making the delegation assignment. Let the person know that this is developmental for them, let them know if this is to get them ready for a higher level assignment, or that it's a training opportunity for them.

The middle section of the delegation guide is extremely important. It outlines specifically what action needs to be taken in order to successfully complete the delegated task. Your role in the process is identified, who else in the organization might need to be involved in completing the task, what budget has been allocated for this task and the time constraints, when is it due. There is space at the bottom for the person to outline briefly options or alternatives to the assigned task that may come up during the delegation process. Basically, you're empowering the person to come back to you and say here are some options or alternatives to the actual delegated task itself. That in itself can be very motivational.

The final section of the discussion guide is an outline of the expected results. This avoids the pitfall of the individual getting halfway through the assignment and reviewing it with you and then finding out that they're on the wrong track. What this section does is outline all the standards, steps, and potential obstacles to what's going to be achieved. And the very last entry sets up the interval for your next meeting and review.

Again, this guide is flexible and adaptable to the situation. Utilize these three overall sections and in varying degrees, depending upon the experience level of the individual, apply each individual component.

So why don't people delegate? To figure out how to delegate properly, it's important to understand why people avoid it. Quite simply, people don't delegate because it takes a lot of up-front effort. After all, which is easier: designing and writing content for a brochure that promotes a new service you helped spearhead, or having other members of your team do it? You know the content inside and out. You can spew benefit statements in your sleep. It would be relatively straightforward for you to sit down and write it. It would even be fun! The question is, "Would it be a good use of your time?"

While on the surface it's easier to do it yourself than explain the strategy behind the brochure to someone else, there are two key reasons that it's probably better to delegate the task to someone else:

1. If you have the ability to spearhead a new campaign, the chances are that your skills are better used further

developing the strategy, and perhaps coming up with other new ideas. By doing the work yourself, you're failing to make best use of your time.

2. By meaningfully involving other people in the project, you develop those people's skills and abilities. This means that next time a similar project comes along, you can delegate the task with a high degree of confidence that it will be done well, with much less involvement from you.

Delegation allows you to make the best use of your time and skills, and it helps other people in the team grow and develop to reach their full potential in the organization.

It reminds me of another quote from Stephen Covey:

"People and organizations don't grow much without delegation and completed staff work because they are confined to the capacities of the boss and reflect both personal strengths and weaknesses."

Let's review when you should or not delegate. Delegation is a win-win when done appropriately, however that does not mean that you can delegate just anything. To determine when delegation is most appropriate there are five key questions you need to ask yourself:

1. Is there someone else who has (or can be given) the necessary information or expertise to complete the task? Essentially is this a task that someone else can do, or is it critical that you do it yourself?
2. Does the task provide an opportunity to grow and develop another person's skills?
3. Is this a task that will recur, in a similar form, in the future?
4. Do you have enough time to delegate the job effectively? Time must be available for adequate training, for questions

and answers, for opportunities to check progress, and for rework if that is necessary.

5. Is this a task that will save you time? Tasks critical for long-term success genuinely do need your attention.

If you can answer, "yes" to at least some of the above questions, then it could well be worth delegating this job.

Once you determine that this is a task that needs to be delegated, and you determine who's the best person to give this assignment to (if you have a choice!), and you complete the delegation guide or use it as a checklist, you can move on to more important tasks that are necessary to keep the business going.

Throughout his business career, Eddie utilized people close to him such as his family and Patsy to help him reach success. It may not always work as well every time you delegate, but remember to build those strong relationships so when you need to delegate, you have the options, the resources, and the people that you can trust to get the job done with your help.

Delegation Discussion Guide	
Topic:	Date:
CONTEXT • Background (facts, history, events, etc.) • Reasons / Rationale for the delegation	
ACTION(S) TO BE TAKEN • Goal • Roles (yours and mine) • People to be involved • Money and other resources allocated or needed • Time constraints • Your recommendations, options, and alternatives	
RESULT(S) EXPECTED • Customer requirements/quality standards to be achieved • Milestone check point dates • Next steps for you • Next steps for me • Potential obstacles Next meeting date/time	

EXCEPTIONAL DIMENSION #10
Perseverance

The key is to identify enemies of perseverance and work to defeat them.
You will be able to rise above to accomplish your loftiest goals.

A pattern starts to develop as we review the characteristics of an *Exceptional Entrepreneur*. Eddie and his life as an entrepreneur demonstrate behaviors that cross over into several different dimensions. Perseverance is one of those dimensions. It touches on resiliency, it impacts the vision, and it takes courage. All these dimensions meld together around this word perseverance.

Let's start with a few basic definitions of perseverance:

• Perseverance is the quality that allows someone to continue trying to do something even though it's difficult.

• Perseverance is the continued effort to do or achieve something despite difficulties, failure, or opposition.

When Eddie set a goal to become the best producer of hamburger meat in the area, he established the essential criteria for demonstrating perseverance, because now he exhibits the dedication, the discipline, and the determination to achieve that goal. And it doesn't happen overnight. You have to stick with it!

Perseverance comes to the forefront when one strives to realize a goal, complete a task, or meet targets by overcoming obstacles. To achieve success one has to develop perseverance. And technically, developing perseverance within one's self is not a difficult task, but it requires effort. *Faith* in one's self and the belief that one can meet a certain goal is one of the most efficient ways in which perseverance can be developed. That's where it starts! In my interview with Patsy Crouch she discusses living with and working with an *Exceptional Entrepreneur* like Eddie. You can see the tremendous faith and confidence that Eddie had in himself and in his vision.

Knowing what obstacles one might have to face in order to achieve a goal can be of great help in sustaining one's effort. Once you gain an understanding of what those obstacles are, one can mentally prepare to meet those obstacles.

To continue to develop perseverance within oneself, one needs to acquire some moral force in support. And this support can come from one's family, a friend, or from some significant influential person. We learned that family was and is a strong motivating force for Eddie and a great support.

Exercising self-control is one of the important aspects needed to develop perseverance. Not losing one's temper, staying the course, not letting emotions get in the way of rational thinking, all contribute to observable self-control and give credence to the maintenance of staying the course.

In addition, it's important that one learns from one's failures as part of developing perseverance. Eddie's effort in the convenience store business is a prime example of learning from one's mistakes. When he outlined the better way of maintaining the financial stability of his stores, treating them as individual entities versus grouping them together under one company, he was exercising this idea of sustaining future efforts by learning from his mistakes.

Perseverance requires determination hence if you take the time and effort to cultivate this tenacity you can achieve the impossible. But there are endless curves or obstacles in the road to success. There are distractions, false beliefs, and a number of components that lead to abandoning what once seemed to be the utmost important target. Here are the 5 greatest enemies of perseverance according *Going Beyond Talent: Eliminating 5 Enemies of Perseverance by The John Maxwell Company.*

1. **A lifestyle of giving up.** If you have a habit of giving up, you need to overcome it to be successful. At times we are programmed to take the easy route. And the easy route might be to give up. However taking the difficult path will allow us to see our talent come to full fruition.

2. **The wrong belief that life should be easy.** It might be common to expect that life should be handed to us on a silver platter but that's not a match with reality. When faced with tough situations, we have two choices. We can either give up or we can dig in and get down in the trenches. Perseverance is choosing the trenches.

3. **A wrong belief that success is a destination**. If you think you have arrived, then you're in trouble. As soon as you think you no longer need to work to make progress, you began to lose ground.

4. **A lack of resiliency.** We can't let discouraging moments break us. Refer to page 105 for *Exceptional Dimension #8 Resilience* to ensure you keep that trait going forward.

5. **A lack of vision.** As an entrepreneur toils in his craft, he sees in his mind's eye what he wants to create or do and keeps working toward it.

Think through these five obstacles or barriers to perseverance and once you identify any of these enemies of perseverance, work on defeating them. You will be able to rise above any situation to accomplish your loftiest goals.

In William J. Bennett's *Book of Virtues*, he devotes a full chapter to perseverance. In his introduction to this virtue, Bennett makes the point that one needs to be a coach and a cheerleader and by witness of our own examples, a model for others to develop perseverance. In this chapter, there are numerous inspirational great works and stories of perseverance from as simple as *Aesop's tail, The Tortoise and the Hare*, to the speech in 1940 by Winston Churchill called *We Shall Fight in the Fields and In the Streets*. There are numerous great speeches and writings that depict the dimension of perseverance. This effort of reading and thinking through these great works is a strong development action you can take to ensure your perseverance is at a peak when and if you approach a career of entrepreneurship or any other leadership role.

EXCEPTIONAL DIMENSION #11
Passion
The key is to follow your heart, but check it with your head!

The successful entrepreneur demonstrates the enthusiasm and excitement for business ventures similar to the way an individual gets excited about riding of roller coaster. The difference is obvious! The roller coaster ride is over quickly. The entrepreneur and his or her passion last for the duration of that business career.

Let's define it: Passion is a strong feeling of enthusiasm for something or about doing something. It's an intense driving feeling or conviction. It can go to an intense emotion compelling some type of action. For most entrepreneurs it's that enthusiasm that is observable and people recognize that enthusiasm. Everyone can see the passion in the entrepreneur's approach to work. It's in the voice, it's in the manner, and it is sustainable. It doesn't go away.

So how do you develop passion? You're not born with it. You can't learn it. It comes from within and represents an unbridled confidence and vision of what you want to accomplish. Or, it can spring from wanting to avoid certain business situations or products or markets. When Eddie determined that he did not want to work for someone, his passion or dream was to be his own boss. By avoiding typical work situations, the entrepreneur drives himself toward being in his own business. What's important is the combination of other characteristics like visionary, dreamer, confidence, and a skill set that can be applied to products and services that clients or customers need or want.

Recently an extensive article in the Wall Street Journal by Mr. Wasserman, a professor at Harvard business school and author of *Anticipating and Avoiding Pitfalls that can Sink a Startup*, spent time outlining some of the dangers of being passionate about what you do. Some of these include:

- Being overconfident and making bad choices at the worst times.

- Being impatient to move forward quickly with too much optimism about potential customers.

- Ignoring market conditions and having their own personal circumstances be overridden by one's passion for getting this business started. They talked themselves into it!

Passion can over shadow the feeling that they are skillful in every area necessary to be successful and build their business. That passion clouds the reality that they may not be prepared or they may not have the connections necessary to launch a new business.

On a personal note, passion for starting a new business and all the optimism that goes with it can take a heavy toll on a family. They may oversell a family member on the potential of the business just to win over their support.

All these dangers can be overcome with a strong dose of reality. Knowing when to launch, knowing the market, knowing the potential demand for their product, can help offset blinding passion. It's not to suggest that the entrepreneur should not have confidence in their dream. They need that enthusiasm to attract investors, employees, and of course customers. It's that balance with reality and doing one's homework.

Effective change management is another tool to splash reality onto the flames of passion. Being flexible and adaptable to changing conditions are extremely important when the entrepreneur faces reality of running his own business. What we're trying to avoid in any changing environment is being caught behind the curve instead of ahead of it. Steven Jobs once said, "Follow your heart, but check it with your head."

A successful entrepreneur follows his/her passion, has a clear vision, identifies common pitfalls, and proactively takes action to avoid unwanted outcomes.

EXCEPTIONAL DIMENSION #12
Positive Attitude
The key is to eliminate any negative mind-talk and just do it!

Another characteristic of a successful entrepreneur is the maintaining of a positive mental attitude toward seeking opportunities. This optimism is characterized best via a strong conviction that demonstrates success.

Those people who were closest to Eddie Crouch consistently speak to his positive mental attitude, his optimistic nature, and total commitment to the business he was in. Patsy, his wife, referred to Eddie's optimism by stating he never thought of any possible failure related to his business ventures. And if things were temporarily derailed, and she was concerned about the future, Eddie would reassure her that everything was going to be fine. And invariable it was!

This character trait, this positivity, is a behavior that can be learned. However, one cannot just attend a class or join a webinar to learn how to be optimistic. It takes practice, repetition, and a true sense of focus to eliminate negative thoughts or pessimistic behavior. In addition, people can observe the positive behavior and adopt the same behavior for themselves. So whether or not you have a model to follow the important first step is to do a self-assessment of your attitude. And, if you're not sure about your behavior, ask people around you how you perform when there is a challenge, a crisis, or some potential problem facing you.

What follows are a series of tips and ideas to start the process of converting any potential pessimism into positive behavior. You can select any one or more of these and begin to focus on the positive aspects of that behavior or avoid the negative aspects of behavior that promotes pessimism.

The following are my **Top 20 tips to Positivity** shared from various resources. You can download this list from our website at www.mlodzikandcrouch.com.

Top 20 tips to Positivity:

1. Remind yourself that most things are possible if you try hard enough.

2. Set a goal to make friends. Eddie had a reputation of never meeting someone that he didn't like. And in most instances the opposite was true also. No one who met Eddie didn't like him. So if you feel you don't have enough of something, such as friends, set a goal to get more of it until you're satisfied.

3. Give everything a chance before you neglect or reject it.

4. Communicate needs. If someone makes you feel negative, tell whomever in a nice way how you feel. Try to fix the problem.

5. Stay upbeat! Don't let other people drag you down. What other people say is always their opinion.

6. Do what makes you happy and isn't harmful.

7. Smile! Smiling is actually proven to keep you happier when you're down or gloomy. So if you're sad, smile! If

you are happy, smile! It makes you a happier person and gives other people a better impression of YOU.

8. Remember that YOU control your attitude. Attitude does not come from what happens to you, but instead from how you decide to interpret what happens.

9. Create a "library" of positive thoughts. If you spend 10 minutes every morning listening to or reading something inspirational or motivational you'll have those thoughts and feelings ready at hand when events don't go exactly the way you'd prefer. It sets a positive tone.

10. Ignore whiners and complainers. These people look at the world through crap- colored glasses! People like this would rather hear you talk about a failure or what's making you miserable then to talk about positive experiences and successes. They are a real drag!

11. Use a more positive vocabulary if you want a positive attitude, your vocabulary must be consistently positive. For example, when someone asks you, "How are you"? Rather than just responding with the standard "Okay, I guess" or "I'm hanging in there", respond with "Terrific!" or "Never better!" and really mean it!

12. Give thanks for each day.

13. Count your personal blessings.

14. Do a good deed without telling anyone. Anonymous giving is the highest form of positive charity.

15. Forgive an old hurt. Holding a grudge for weeks, months or even years can sour the expression on one's face.

16. Compliment someone.

17. Admire the view!

18. Donate something.

19. Volunteer to help the needy.

20. Frame events in a positive way. Your beliefs about life and work determine how you interpret events, and therefore your attitude. There is a verse on page 61 of this book called *Living Life* that exemplifies this practice. Plus, as so often happened with Eddie, when something would go wrong it would open up another opportunity. For example, when one of Crouch Meat's largest customers challenged Eddie and Patsy with a difficult order, Eddie was already working on the solution before the conversation was actually completed. That's because he saw this challenge as an opportunity to demonstrate his company's ability to respond and provide outstanding service.

These ideas or tips will not fit everyone specifically, so select, modify, and adopt positive behaviors. Over time, positivity will resonate with the people around you. Successful entrepreneurs and great leaders of all kinds are people who have mastered the ability to communicate positivity and set a clear path for their own success, overcoming obstacles, solving problems, and keeping a close eye on a very positive future.

Conclusion

This book recounts the life of Eddie Crouch, the *Exceptional Entrepreneur*. The intent is to demonstrate that life events and relationships often shape the character traits needed to succeed in business. For example, Eddie's father demonstrated many of the behaviors that Eddie observed and adopted as his own. The "Early Business Years" section exhibits how Eddie's behaviors impacted his career, business, and his life.

Throughout Eddie's story, I have highlighted the *12 Exceptional Dimensions* that have contributed to his success and when developed are key attributes for others who want to succeed in business. However, there are other characteristics, talents and skills that have not been covered in this book that should be considered. For example, financial acumen is an important component that we touch on but is not related to the dimensions or behaviors of this text.

My goal is that you will use this book as guide to assess your opportunities for success in starting a business venture and/or to become a great leader and apply the tools and techniques outlined in each of the *Exceptional Dimensions* to create a development plan that will further enhance and contribute to success in your current position or in your future career, no matter what field you pursue.

Good luck in your endeavors!

About the Author

Ed Mlodzik

Ed Mlodzik is a student of Leadership. Ed began his "calling" as a high school teacher in Dayton, Ohio. He then joined the Bell System as their Training Manager where he taught sales, management, and product courses. He transferred to United Telephone Company in Kansas City to become their Training Manager. United eventually acquired a long distance telecommunications company that evolved into Sprint. There he focused on the Management and Leadership Development curriculum mastering the principles, techniques, and tools that strengthen the leadership skills. He helped create an internal Executive Coaching program and lead a group of nine coaches who worked with executives and managers to increase their effectiveness.

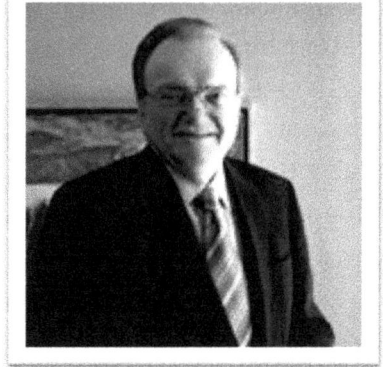

Ed Mlodzik and Eddie Crouch became fast friends several years ago. Coined as the *Exceptional Entrepreneur*, Ed recognized the power of Eddie's story and wrote this book as a guide to help others develop the skills and behaviors to achieve success. Whether you are just starting a business or want to develop as a leader, this book will steer you in the direction needed to turn your dreams into reality.

About the Exceptional Entrepreneur

Eddie Crouch

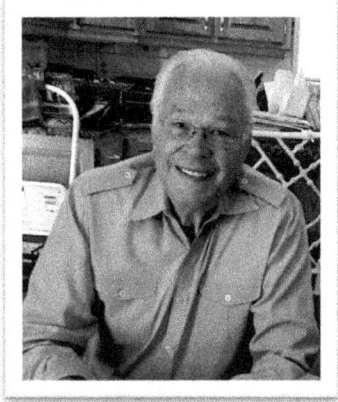

Eddie Crouch is the *Exceptional Entrepreneur!* Passion, positivity, perseverance and faith guided Eddie's journey, never letting fear deter him from his dreams. He says, "It never entered my mind to think of failure!"

Eddie started exercising his competencies as a young boy working hard at school and with his father. He began his career at an early age and rose to success in the beef business. He is an active member of his church and spends his free time restoring old cars. He lives in the house he built in Kansas and is *living life* with his wife, Patsy, and pup, Peanut. Eddie's close-knit family, his dear friends, and neighbors in the community, continue to be an important part of his blessed life.

Eddie is a proud and giving man that continues to share his generosity with his family!

References

The following are resources referenced in the book and also suggested readings to aid in your development plan.

It's Your Ship by Michael Abrashoff

The Book of Virtues by William J. Bennett

Execution by Bossidy & Charan

Good to Great by Jim Collins

First Things First by Steven R. Covey and A. Roger Merrill

The 7 Habits if Highly Effective People by Steven R. Covey

The 8th Habit by Steven R. Covey

The Executive Handbook by Gebelein, Lee, & Sloan of Personnel Decisions International

Recapturing The Spirit of Enterprise by George Gilder

Seabiscuit and *Unbroken* by Laura Hillenbrand

The Five Dysfunctions of a Team by Patrick Lencioni

Silos, Politics, & Turf Wars by Patrick Lencioni

Beyond Talent: Becoming Someone that Gets Extraordinary Results and *Going Beyond Talent: Eliminating 5 Enemies of Perseverance* by The John Maxwell Company.

www.ingramcontent.com/pod-product-compliance
Lightning Source LLC
Chambersburg PA
CBHW071601200326
41519CB00021BB/6834